CONTENTS

IV. LOOKING AHEAD

FOREWORD

BY SHARON SALZBERG

This is a book about beginnings—the spiritual beginnings of teenagers, of adults now in their twenties and thirties, and of some well-known Buddhists who look back over the decades to their early years of Buddhist practice. There is a moment, for all of us, when the threads of our conditioning and interactions and experiences and influences come together in a certain way, and our spiritual journey is launched. The suffering we have gone through, the inspiration we have been lifted by, the doors we have seen opening before us embolden us to leave the convenient and familiar, and venture forth.

My own journey began, as it does for so many others, in college. At a young age, I lost both my parents, and was raised by a succession of family members. I spent most of my time hiding my feelings, or distorting them, so that no one would really know how sad I was. When I was sixteen, I enrolled at the State University of New York at Buffalo. When I heard about an Asian philosophy course on Buddhism, I signed up, and discovered that the only time I really came alive was for an hour and a half on Tuesdays and Thursdays during that class. As time went on, and I learned more about the Buddha's teaching, I found myself beginning to wonder if I too might one day be truly happy. Maybe there was a path to freedom from suffering after all.

When I learned about a junior-year-abroad program, I felt ready to leave everything in order to travel to India, a place about which I knew nothing, in the hopes that I might learn to meditate. The discovery of the practical tools of meditation and the liberating path of Buddhism proved to be a compelling life direction from which I have never turned away.

Over the last thirty years, I have met other like-minded practitioners along the way who are beginning a spiritual path. Their friendship, encouragement, and advice have made all the difference in my own search. Reading the essays in this book is like an encounter with spiritual friends—friends whose support and shared stories affirm our own experience, opening us to the uniqueness of our own path.

I first met Sumi Loundon when she was sixteen, at a time when few young adults came through the doors of the meditation center where I teach in Barre, Massachusetts. Today, a noticeable proportion of those attending retreats and working on staff at the Insight Meditation Society is under forty, reflecting a new generational wave in American Dharma centers overall. The sincerity and energy of these young seekers is refreshing. Likewise, this timely anthology is full of the eagerness and curiosity with which we begin our spiritual journey. Sumi has gathered wonderful reflections here, which range from the tentative first steps of teens laying down their first thoughts on paper to the thoughtfulness of the distinguished teachers who lend their voices to this collection.

I have delighted in the playfulness and power of these diverse stories, and hope this book serves as a special companion in your own path to awakening.

EDITOR'S PREFACE

Seven years ago, while cooking and cleaning as a volunteer at a small New England meditation center, it dawned on me that I was surrounded by people of my parents' generation. Our conversations revolved around reminiscences of the '60s, children leaving for college, and retirement plans. Where were all the people my age, the twenty-somethings? I certainly wasn't encountering them here—so I went looking for them. I set out on an email and telephone journey leading to the discovery that, happily, Buddhism would not pass away with the baby-boomer generation. I met hundreds of young adults who were not, as I imagined they might be, superficial in their exploration of the Buddhist tradition. Rather, their energy for transforming their lives and the world's communities was sincere, fresh, and unbounded.

I was struck that most of these young spiritual seekers felt as alone and isolated in their Dharma path as I had. If they were fortunate enough to live close to a meditation center or temple, they, like me, were often the youngest by decades. Yet most weren't even that fortunate. The majority lived in families and communities that had little connection to traditions other than Christianity. Young adults had to figure out for themselves what they were spiritually hungry for and find what they needed. We found that being in conversation with even one person, each other, opened up a rich world of peer learning. Simply to be affirmed in our questions was encouraging.

We discovered that we all struggle with the issue of our own identity. Identity issues around personality, profession, and lifestyle typify the young adult years. But these young people are also wrestling with stepping into a spiritual world that, while not exactly counterculture, is not mainstream either. For many, there are few ways of exploring and forming their religious identity outside their own personal study. Looking back on it, I realize that one of my own motivations for reaching out to other young seekers was that I also was wrestling to find who I was and who I wanted to become. Getting to know my generation has helped me discover a sense of identity in the context of the larger Buddhist community.

Seeing that we had loneliness and the search for identity in common, I realized we needed to form a support community for ourselves. If sharing stories had done so much for me, then why not offer these stories to other young adults, too? Giving expression to these explorations in Buddhism gave rise to an anthology, *Blue Jean Buddha: Voices of Young Buddhists,* in 2001. Through their own personal stories, young Buddhists reflected on how Dharma teachings addressed depression, drugs, relationships, living in the city, and technology. Some wrote about spiritual practices, such as sitting a meditation retreat, praying with Tibetans in India, calling on Amida Buddha, and being assisted out of danger by the active compassion of the *bodhisattva* Tara. Others explored their unfolding path as social activists, hospice workers, athletes, and monastics.

As *Blue Jean Buddha* brought me into contact with greater numbers of young Buddhists both here in America and in other parts of the world, it became clear that there were many other rich, wonderful stories to be shared. Most especially, and perhaps because I was still getting a basic orientation for myself as an early twenty-something, I had overlooked the stories of teenagers. A few teenagers emailed with some variant of, "I liked your book, but what about us?" I had assumed teenagers would have little to say, with necessarily just a few years of the spiritual journey behind them. Yet, as I began truly engaging teen-aged Buddhists, it became clear that they have an interest in and ability to thoughtfully explore a spiritual path.

I also received letters from older Buddhists. The essays by young Buddhists stimulated some to reflect on their own early years. I found these retrospectives compelling because in many respects they mirrored the stories from my generation. It was affirming to hear that those older adults had gone through the confusion and questioning I was experiencing. Taken together, their stories provided the perspective that what I and other young adults were going through were not permanent states of uncertainty, as many of us feared, but necessary stages in the unfolding of a life. What a relief! And so the third section of this book comprises the stories of longtime Buddhists looking back on their early years.

As I have gotten to know more young Buddhists over these past few years, one of the most frequently raised topics of discussion has been about relationships. Actually, make that *the* most frequently discussed topic. While *Blue Jean Buddha* had a few stories about boyfriends, girlfriends, parents, and teachers, it became clear that young people wanted to hear more. The young adult years are marked by tectonic shifts in our relationships, as we leave our parents, search for partners, consider commitment and perhaps marriage, leave home towns and find new communities through college, workplaces, and temples. Those who are taking up a Buddhist path naturally think about how Dharma teachings guide us in changing old relationships and forming new ones with skill, wisdom, and compassion. For that reason, this book devotes half a section to exploring the interface between relationships and the Dharma life.

The second half of the section from those in their twenties and thirties addresses the dimensions of Buddhist practice. The essays are not in any way meant to be a "how to" of Dharma practice, but rather, these are a portrayal of what actually happens in a young person's spiritual life, the kinds of questions we encounter, and how we tackle problems. The contributors explore the path of practice, how it twists and turns, takes us into unknown territory, and challenges our expectations.

These first three sections are arranged by age group, beginning with essays by teenagers, followed by stories from those in their twenties and thirties on practice and relationships, and concluding with the reflections of longtime Buddhists on their youth. Through this arrangement, I hope to provide a rough sketch of how the spiritual life matures and the Buddhist path ripens. One point of this arrangement is to reassure younger readers that everything they're going through builds on itself and is necessary and useful.

I have wondered whether some readers might be compelled to compare themselves against the stories. Perhaps it is helpful to recognize that most of the contributors in this anthology, while young, are not beginners and have been invested in Buddhist practice for a number of years. In some ways, these writers do not represent those young people who are presently beginning to explore Buddhism (although most describe how they got started on their path). At the same time, the essays represent some of the major issues that we all think about growing up and finding our spirituality. I hope readers will simply start from where they are, take what's useful, and leave the rest without comparing.

With each piece, the given age is the age at the time of writing. Because of the necessarily long process of bringing a book into being, many of the contributors' biographies, and dispositions towards Buddhism, have changed. For this reason, the writings here can be understood as a snapshot of each contributor's views at that particular period in his or her life.

In the fourth and final section I step back from the world of young Buddhists to look at larger issues. Reflecting on my own experiences as a young Buddhist, and drawing from the thoughts of many others, I would like to address how we can better support young people in Buddhism. Organizers in Buddhist communities have recently begun to think about actively engaging young people. What is needed to help the next generation develop? What can young Buddhists themselves do to encourage each other? How might longtime Buddhists play a role?

This book begins to fill what I see is a gap in today's Dharma literature. We have shelves of wonderful books on Buddhism, meditation, and philosophy but we have little on the actual practices and beliefs of contemporary Buddhists. For some, this is a powerful way of learning. It is also an especially important way for young people, who are naturally inclined to learn through mutual exploration with peers. Many young people are not able to connect with local Dharma communities in person: they might be in an area without a group, such as a rural, Midwestern town; they may not be able to drive or have access to a car; they might not have parental support; or they might feel shy about entering a group on their own. A book like this can, I hope, provide a literary *sangha,* a community of peers through which one can further understand oneself.

Someone told me recently that a current fad on some college campuses is "slacklining." "What's that?" I asked, imagining it as a combination of, somehow, being a slacker and mainlining. "It's like tightrope walking, except the line is slack. It develops concentration and feels like meditation," my friend explained. I immediately thought, "I should have had an essay on slacklining in this anthology. I wonder if I'm missing any other trends." This moment pointed to the impossibility of capturing every demographic and sentiment of the young Buddhist experience in one, two, or even ten anthologies. *Blue Jean Buddha* in some way laid out the breadth of young peoples' experiences. This book is intended to go into greater depth about how we young people think about our Buddhist life.

Sumi Loundon

Barre, Massachusetts

Summer 2005

ACKNOWLEDGMENTS

This book would not have been possible without the generous efforts of many good people. For a second time, the dedicated staff of Wisdom Publications has been essential to bringing an anthology by young Buddhists into being. I am especially indebted to my editor, Josh Bartok, to the publisher, Tim McNeill, and to Rod Meade Sperry, the publicist. Kai Lee Loundon, my brother, and Connie Pham, an insightful young woman in California whom I know only through email, read through drafts of every essay and provided excellent feedback. Franz Metcalf and Lodro Rinzler gave thoughtful advice on the last chapter. These three were critical to the development of this book. Paul Morris, Diana Winston, Soren Gordhamer, Claudie Haydon (Heiman), and David Zuniga, contributors to the first anthology, and Jeff Wilson, Kathleen Olesky, and Alexis Walker (Trass) of this anthology, were always on hand as impromptu consultants. I am grateful to the many teenagers and young adults—in America, Canada, England, Australia, Peru, Malaysia, Singapore, Thailand, Korea, Japan, and other countries—who have shared their life stories with me. Likewise, I appreciate the counsel of countless older and longtime Buddhists who told their stories and put things into perspective.

Although many stories from young and older alike could not be included in this volume, their experiences have shaped the vision for this anthology.

I am truly grateful to each of the contributors in this volume, who worked hard on their essays and who are allowing their candid stories to be shared with the public. I owe many thanks to the longtime Buddhist contributors, who are busy Dharma teachers and leaders in their communities, for their time and support. I am indebted to Sharon Salzberg for writing the foreword and for her enthusiasm for this work. Likewise, many thanks to the Buddhist Biggies who kindly wrote endorsements. The staff and Dharma teachers of the greater Insight community in Barre, Massachusetts, have been wonderfully supportive of this project in many seen and unseen ways. Finally, I bow to my husband Ilmee Hwansoo Kim whose understanding of the Buddhist tradition provided invaluable perspective. His kindness, generosity, and sincerity make being on the path together joyful.

SECTION I
Teens

"*I Try*"

HILARY MILLER

My parents walked slowly through the art gallery, studying each piece, even the ones that didn't seem to have much to offer, with care. I trailed sullenly after them. An artist myself, I usually enjoyed looking at paintings and sculptures, but there was nothing here that even remotely spoke to me.

"*Now* can we go?" I begged my parents, sounding more adolescent than I would like to admit.

"Be patient," my mom said.

My dad was more direct. "You know, in a situation like this, you should just walk and breathe." He put his hand firmly under my chin and turned my head so that I was looking up at him. "This is true meditation," he continued. I angrily jerked my head away. I hated it when my dad told me things about practice, as if he knew more about it than I did. I snarled back, "And do you practice mindfulness all the time?"

"I try."

His response was simple and honest. I was still angry, but I felt quieter. As I became calmer, the moment left me with a revelation

Hilary Miller, 14, practices Chan Buddhism and enjoys working with horses.

3

about my father. Suddenly, his advice about meditating no longer felt threatening.

My dad was my door to Buddhism—and a mirror of myself as well. I was twelve when he opened the door, though it took me a while to walk through.

We were driving home in his new Miata, still full of that new-car smell. His newly bought books were stacked on my lap. "What are they about?" I asked, for lack of anything better to say.

"Zen," he said.

"Oh . . . what's Zen?"

"It's a form of Buddhism, a very pure form. It was created in an attempt to go back to the original teachings of the Buddha."

I looked with more interest at the glossy covers of the books.

To me, Buddhism was what I had learned about in my religions survey class: all life is suffering so go sit on a mountain and meditate on ants. About two months later, I examined our bookshelves and found a row of about twelve books on Zen. A month after that, I actually opened one. It was radically different from what I thought Buddhism was. Many of the teachings just felt right. Still, I wasn't comfortable with the bleak style of Zen my dad favored. It seemed like a stark practice, with Zen masters who, rather than speaking, gave their students a good whack or chopped a cat in two. Thus, I shied away from Charlotte Joko Beck's spare writing on bare awareness and moved toward Thich Nhat Hanh's emphasis on peace and love. It was after I read *Touching Peace* that I really felt drawn to practice.

After eight months, I had an altar in my room, was meditating regularly, and I wore a *mala,* a Buddhist rosary, on my wrist. My parents and I never talked about it, but they must have heard my bell-ringing in the mornings and my chanting. An unvoiced acknowledgment hung in the air between us, and I was comfortable with that. I almost felt that, were I or anyone else to make a fuss about my Buddhist practice, it would become somehow less real.

But another thing went unvoiced: a silent conflict between my dad and me. I'm not sure if he was aware of this conflict, but there were times when I burned with anger. He would order me, "Go meditate," and inwardly I would explode with fury. In fact, I probably *should* have gone and meditated at those times, like he told me, but I didn't hear the message. My pesky ego wouldn't be quiet long enough for me to think about it. All I knew was that he was imposing on what was mine. How dare he presume to tell me what to do in my spiritual life? I was *practicing* what he had only read about!

One time, I snapped at him, "You read all these books on Buddhism, but you never actually apply them to your life!" He looked at me and said, "You think they haven't affected the way I think? The way I act?" I was startled into silence. I pushed the incident into the back of my mind, but it lingered there until finally, in the art gallery, it evolved into a realization about my father.

The words "I try" made me realize that my dad wasn't just reading about Buddhism. It helped me to understand that he was a Buddhist in practice, too, just in a different way than I was. He never called himself Buddhist, and I don't think he even thought of himself as one. But I'm sure that there were elements of the Buddha's teachings that he grasped much more fully than I did.

After that moment in the gallery, I also realized I was becoming lost in the rituals, in all the pretty colors of Buddhism. My dad brought me back to simple practice, back to the everyday. Sitting on the cushion in my room, I worked past my anger and it became clear to me that he was giving me a gift. I tried to practice mindfulness, but often I forgot. Why should I resent his reminding me? In this way, he was my mirror.

The day following the incident in the gallery, we were walking and I asked him, "Have you ever considered meditating? You have the time, now that you aren't working."

He was silent a few moments. Finally, he said, "I've thought about it. But I still don't know whether I can make that commitment."

The path I walk is very much my own. Yet in that moment, it seemed to me that with our very different angles on Buddhism, my father and I had something to offer each other. In a strange and wonderful way, we keep each other in balance.

"Yes, I'm a Buddhist"

ANNE SKUZA

"What happened that day may have been the result of *karma*..." blared a television documentary in my grandma's upper-middle-class living room in Gdansk, a Polish port city on the Baltic Sea. My grandmother turned down the program and asked loudly, "*Karma*. Now that's a Buddhist word, isn't it?"

"Um, yes, I believe it is," I said.

"I've heard that *you've* become interested in Buddhism."

"Well, yes, you could say that."

"Hmph, never had much respect for that Buddha fellow. Always thought of him a disgusting, slothful pasha."

"What makes you say that, grandma?"

"Wasn't he a prince and all, never doing any work, having figures of himself made of gold?"

"Well, he was a prince at first, but then renounced that, choosing first the ascetic path and then the Middle Way."

"Hmph, maybe so. Now don't you go mixing with those foreign fanatics! Changing one's religion never brought anybody any happiness. It's unnatural."

Anne Skuza, 13, was drawn to Buddhism after studying it in a world religions class in school.

And with that closing remark from my grandmother I gave up any hope of visiting the local Tibetan Buddhist temple during my summer vacation in Gdansk.

My quest for enlightenment began nearly two years ago when I stumbled onto Dinty W. Moore's *The Accidental Buddhist* at the public library, while looking for an appealing religious philosophy to replace the one I was raised in. The religion of many Poles, including my family, is Catholic, with a healthy smattering of ancient pagan superstitions. For many, including me, one is Christian solely because one's parents and grandparents were Catholic, and not because of any personal conviction. I, a searching eleven-year-old, set out to break that mold by finding a religion I could truly believe in. I scoured the library but was disappointed to initially find nothing that spoke to me, except *The Accidental Buddhist*. I finished the book in one night of rapid page-turning and was instantly hooked. Once I checked out and read nearly every Buddhist book in the library: I read Sogyal Rinpoche's *The Tibetan Book of Living and Dying* and Lama Surya Das' *Awakening the Buddha Within* so intensively that the books were soon so worn they were almost unreturnable.

I turned to the Internet. In addition to finding down-to-earth advice and practical teachings, I was able to communicate with a Buddhist community greater than the virtually nonexistent one in my town. It comforted me to know that I wasn't the only one searching for my purpose in life.

As you can imagine, my parents' reactions to my explorations where similar to my grandmother's. Initially they rationalized my new-found faith as just a passing phase, but as the months rolled by and I showed no intention of growing tired of Buddhism, they began to genuinely worry. Many Europeans and Americans imagine Buddhism as a relic of the psychedelic, drug-crazed '60s and '70s or look upon it as intensely foreign. My parents were afraid that I would shave my head, start taking drugs, or become a vegan. They were afraid that I would become the family weirdo, bringing nothing but embarrassment to the family name. But after a few difficult discussions, my parents finally recognized that no harm was coming to me and began to tolerate my beliefs.

Buddhism has played a positive role in my life so far. I'm less stressed, happier, and more content with myself. I'm better able to deal with my emotions. I'm not implying, though, that my life as a Buddhist has been all sunshine! Last winter, after reading a book on the transience of life, I felt as if my existing had no real point. I felt and spoke like a madwoman. Then I realized that since I worked so hard in my past lives to get a human reincarnation, I shouldn't spend time negatively dwelling on it and wasting it; I should celebrate it. When I look back at that incident now, I realize that I went a bit too fast, especially without the guidance of an experienced Buddhist teacher, and that I was misconstruing the teachings on emptiness.

While I've been on the Buddhist path I've had my ups and downs—periods when I felt intensely Buddhist, and periods when I've felt detached from all religions in general. I've weathered those, however, and now feel at ease replying to those who ask, "Yes, I'm a Buddhist." …Well, perhaps not to my grandmother. With her, I've learned to be less direct, so I have strategically "lost" a copy of *Awakening the Buddhist Heart* in her house. Not long ago, I caught a glimpse of her actually looking through it, perhaps reading about that pasha, the Buddha.

The Fuss Over Suffering

J. MARION

At first, I did not understand why Buddhism made such a big fuss over suffering. I was growing up in a comfortable, middle-class family and hadn't personally experienced very much that I would identify as suffering. But the Buddha's first noble truth became real to me my senior year of high school.

I had a full academic schedule and enough extracurricular activities to keep me busy well into the next decade. I was also beginning the daunting task of searching for the perfect college and the financial aid to get me there. In the midst of all this, I managed to find spare moments, usually before collapsing into bed, to practice some breathing meditation or say a few quick Kuan Yin *mantras*. My schedule was full, but I was content.

In late fall, I noticed that a good friend of mine was suddenly changing her appearance and attitude—she looked more and more distressed. Usually Caitlin* knew how to put on a good show, acting so cool and confident that I never would have

---

J. Marion, 19, *a practitioner of the Pure Land tradition, is a student at the University of South Florida, majoring in religious studies.*

* Some names changed in this essay and throughout this book.

guessed that a problem had been building for months. I asked her about what was going on. She confessed that she was depressed and having thoughts of suicide. She said not to worry because her parents were taking care of her. Caitlin begged me not to say a word to anyone because she didn't want others to spread rumors or think badly of her. I agreed, reluctantly. After all, I reasoned, she was just coming off a medication that affected her hormones and, if her family was taking care of her, what choice did I have but to honor her request?

While Caitlin was struggling, my own home life was getting bad. My parents were going through a less-than-amicable divorce and things were tense. I tried to find a middle ground so that I could be loyal to both sides, but inevitably, things did not always work out that way. With Caitlin's troubles and my parents' divorce, I tried to manage by sincerely applying what I knew about the Dharma to both situations. I worked at keeping my *bodhisattva* vows and engaged in meditation daily. I became frustrated, however, because I didn't feel as though I was making any progress. The idea of giving up the path crossed my mind more than once.

By early winter, Caitlin had become much worse, no matter how hard I tried to help her. She seemed determined to self-destruct. One evening, we were talking on the phone and she was distraught and angry at the world. In the background, I could hear her mother pleading to talk with her. Caitlin got angrier and angrier. Suddenly, at the peak of her anger and distress, while her mom had stepped out of the room to get her father, Caitlin threatened over the phone to kill herself. I pleaded with her continuously to reconsider, trying to buy time until her mother could come back to rescue her. (Earlier in the fall, Caitlin had tried to end her life but failed, so I believed it was crucial for me to stay on the phone to calm her down.) Suddenly I heard her cry out and there was a struggle. Her mom had reentered the room and saw immediately what was going on. She wrestled a razor away from Caitlin's hands.

My heart ached for her but there was not much more I could do. Hanging up the phone, I lit a candle before my tiny image of Kuan Yin, Bodhisattva of Compassion, and prayed that everything would work out for the best. My daily prayers having steadily declined over the fall, it was now rare for me to even face the little altar in my bedroom, let alone utter a bodhisattva's name. I think my prayer worked, though, as a few days later Caitlin was hospitalized and could finally receive the care she needed.

With Caitlin safe, I was able to refocus on my home life. My relationship with my family was in need of help. By early spring I lost count of the number of arguments and disagreements. I was very frustrated with the entire situation and felt like there was nothing I could do. I also didn't care very much at this point about my spiritual life. I felt cut off from it and filled the empty feeling with tons of activities. I spent hours everyday after school in meetings for clubs and rehearsals for the drama society. I would go from there to dance class and return home late at night. Just before bed, I would do several hours of homework.

By mid-spring of my senior year, I was feeling so overwhelmed that I became aware of my real suffering. One afternoon, feeling especially miserable, I remembered the teaching about the six realms of existence. I began to understand why those on the lower paths don't care to learn or practice the teachings—like me, they are too exhausted! I also began to grasp how profound the bodhisattva vows were. That short prayer I said to Kuan Yin many months before was more significant than I understood at the time. It expressed a pure aspiration from my heart for healing and happiness for someone other than me.

Around the same time that I came back to these teachings, a wise friend came into my life, my bodhisattva. I had known my bodhisattva for some time but it was not until this point in time that I started listening to her advice, or more accurately, I was able to hear her. She did not expound some great *sutra* or the teachings of an *arahat*. Instead, she simply quoted an old Beatles song, "Let It Be." All of sudden I understood. I felt like the student who in an instant finally got the old master's *koan*. From that moment things began to change. I did not wake up the next day totally free from suffering. Instead, I woke up remembering that we have the ability to change our *karma* and our minds.

It was through my friend that I was able to come into full contact with Kuan Yin. My friend's compassion and wisdom helped bring me full circle out of the sorrowful place I was mired in and back to Dharma. In her, I could see the reflection of a million Buddhas. To my bodhisattva friend I am forever grateful.

Toward the end of the school year things were finally calm. Caitlin was in and out of the hospital and we eventually lost contact with each other. My family life improved and I was reinvigorated in my practice. I even began Buddha recitation again, which ironically had been my central practice and yet the first thing I stopped practicing.

At first I was resentful about the turmoil of my senior year, thinking I was robbed of something. The more I thought about it, though, the greater the gratitude I felt. I now realize that everything was really part of the Way.

When I reflect on what has gotten me from there to here, I think of two things: the Great Bodhisattva Vows that carried me through my senior year and the two phrases I now carry with me every day, "Namo Kuan Shi Yin" and "Namo Amitabha!"

The Little Things in Life

MAYA PUTRA

I've grown as a Buddhist through the little things rather than big moments in life. Several years ago, I bought an *NSYNC CD at a bargain. One of my friends really liked that album and had a copy of it herself. However, she wasn't satisfied with her CD because it was an illegal copy and couldn't be played on the computer, as mine could. One day, while I wasn't looking, she slipped my enhanced CD into her CD case and put another CD on top, hoping I wouldn't see it—but I did. Even though I noticed that she'd done this, I couldn't bring myself to confront her about it because I didn't know for sure if it was in fact my CD in there. After she left, I checked my CD case and saw that mine was missing. I began to cry, not because I had been duped or lost my CD, but because I was sorry she made such a foolish decision. Had she the courage to ask me, I would have willingly given it to her as I never really fancied *NSYNC to begin with. Later, I decided to call and confront her. She denied the whole thing, claiming that I had wrongly accused her. Not wanting to start a fight, I let it go.

Maya Putra, 15, a vipassana student active in the Houston Indonesian Buddhist Association, enjoys filmmaking and being a member of social and environmental advocacy organizations.

The next day she came over to give me a compensatory gift. At the door, I told her that I still believed she took my CD and that she could keep it if she'd like. She became angry with me, said that she never wanted anything to do with me, and then left. When I opened the gift, I found the counterfeit CD inside. Seeing that this was not mine, I returned it to her with a note saying something like, "Thank you for your generous offer, but I do not want to take what is not rightfully mine. Even though you might not consider me as a friend, I will always consider you to be one."

That evening, she came over again, this time with my enhanced CD. She apologized and I forgave her. A few months later I gave the CD to her as a birthday present and never touched that subject again. These little interactions help me grow as a Buddhist.

Growing up in Indonesia for eight years, I was raised as a Buddhist. My mom was my greatest influence: she brought me to Sunday school and taught me most of everything I now know about Buddhism through a series of Jataka tales, stories of the Buddha's past lives. As a little kid, the Buddha was a role model for me, and when I ran into trouble, I would ask myself, "How would Buddha handle this situation?" As I grew older, I became interested in meditation, especially the technique taught by S. N. Goenka called *vipassana*. Through vipassana, I have become more aware of myself, my relationships with people, and the environment. A few years ago, I took two meditation courses. I found them very challenging, because they required ten days of "noble silence" and self-observation. I appreciated the fact that the food and accommodation were free and that the courses welcomed everyone, including non-Buddhists.

How delightful it is to know the Dhamma in this ever-stressful society of ours! I maintain a vipassana practice at least once a day and occasionally sit with a small group on Mondays. After having taken the vipassana course, I'm more aware of what I do, physically as well as mentally. I can immediately recognize any slight changes in my mood. Furthermore, I am able to catch myself before unpleasant feelings take over. Seeing them clearly, they diminish. My parents have noticed I have a greater degree of self-control.

Buddhism has also helped me become aware of the importance of conserving nature and protecting the environment. I'm currently an active member of the Student Environmental Art Council (SEAC).

Recently, I attended an art and science camp sponsored by SEAC and a few other organizations. And at that camp, there were tons of mosquitoes swarming around just waiting for the right moment to suck the victim's juicy blood. That summer, the inflicting West Nile Virus mosquitoes were making headlines. Most of my friends would swat the mosquitoes erratically, killing most of them, which I found to be somewhat disturbing. In my opinion, killing mosquitoes is not a solution because more are bound to come your way and by the time you know it, you'll be slapping yourself endlessly. I was certainly not going to be the one suffering, so I decided it would be best to apply insect repellent. Not only did this guarantee my body to be bug free, but also it was another way to avoid killing them. Instead of swatting them, I would try to generate compassion for one of nature's smaller beings and accept their nature of blood sucking as a way of survival. Who's to say that mosquitoes are making my life miserable? I believe misery is only found within one's mind.

Buddhism has truly made an impact on my wish to make this world a better place for all beings.

The Internet plays a big role in my religious growth. I'm somewhat of an Internet geek and spend between ten to twenty hours a week online. I chat on various servers such as IRC, Yahoo, MSN, AA, and ICQ. Recently, I've been chatting on "Buddhist Chat 1" because this is one of the few rooms where people don't use vulgar references. Some of the topics the room discusses are the difference between good and evil, reincarnation (which always provokes controversy!), evolution versus religion, and the different techniques of meditation. The participants vary in practice such as Nichiren, Dzogchen, Pure Land, Mahayana, and Theravada. Age groups also vary from teenagers to senior citizens—usually I'm the youngest.

I am also a member of a few Internet clubs, one of which is called "DhammaCakraTra_US" in Yahoo. This group is aimed at Indonesian Buddhists and currently consists of 97 Indonesians living in the U.S., 26 of which are Houstonians. Occasionally, we have gatherings when those 26 members including myself pray together and listen to taped lectures. This gives Indonesian Buddhists within the Greater Houston area a chance to expand their Buddhist understanding and hold Dhamma discussions in our own Indonesian language.

I feel I can develop the intellectual side of Buddhism through dialogues with people. There's one person with whom I used to discuss sutras. Through passages of the sutras we've grown so much in Dhamma and in fact he has become one of my closest friends, even closer than those I see daily. Recently, this friend of mine has been suffering from leukemia, and I have been prostrating in front of the altar praying for his welfare ever since I learned of this.

Although this experience has been difficult to cope with, my friend's battle against death has made me more appreciative of life and the things I have. In the past I used to take the little things for granted. Never did it occur to me that I might just die tomorrow. Now I've made it a daily exercise to tell my loved ones, especially my mom and dad, how much I love, appreciate, and respect them.

That Sighing Feeling

ANDREW B. HOWK

Take a deep breath, hold it in for as long as you can, then sigh. This is the only way I can describe to someone who has never lived through depression what every day is like. (Though many teens might argue that's what it can feel like to be a teenager.) The key difference between depression and stress is that depression continues unremittingly. Day after day, week after week, it is relentless in its pressure. Every now and then everything will be all right, the world will seem sane, yet I quickly lose my glimmer of hope and the sinking, sighing feeling returns.

I often lived with a horrible sense that I was missing something key in my life. Even more horrible, I didn't know what that something was. I would later find out that that "thing" was *meaning*. I had lost sight of the "why" to my life. My specific condition was hard for everyone around me to believe since I had become a master of disguise. I, like most with some sort of depression, had adapted to my situation by perfecting a way of projecting what I wanted to be and convincing those around me to think that's what I really was. The truth, though, was that I

Andrew B. Howk, 17, founded the online forum Teen Buddhist Sangha.

was scared and falling fast. Rock bottom became a not-so-distant stop for me as drugs, alcohol, and other escapes began to consume more and more of my life. Just when I thought there was no reason to want any more out of life than the fulfillment of these escapes, my miracle happened.

I was walking though the local library and for whatever reason wandered into the religion section. I must have been careless since somehow I managed to knock a book out onto the floor. When I reached down and began to read what was on the pages something instantly clicked. The words in print began to fill the void that I had created in my life. They spoke of meaning and purpose to life—topics I had all but given up on. What was this wonderful philosophy that could turn my life around? Buddhism. I was shocked. Like many Americans, the closest I had ever come to knowing the Dharma was the nearest Chinese restaurant with its Happy Buddha statue. In my mind, the Buddha was the name of that fat guy who greeted visitors with a smile, not the founder and teacher of something that could rip me back to reality.

The book I knocked off the library shelves was *The Heart of the Buddha's Teaching* by Thich Nhat Hanh. After reading his elegant, meaningful words, I was hooked. From then on—from *That's Funny, You Don't Look Buddhist* by Sylvia Boorstein and *Awakening the Buddha Within* by Lama Surya Das to the wealth of books by the Dalai Lama—you name it, I read it. Bookstores, libraries, the Internet—anything and everything I could access the Dharma through I absorbed like a sponge. I was initially hesitant to refer to Buddhism as a religion since the term held not-so-pleasant memories from my early childhood.

The point when I absolutely knew without a doubt that I had found something genuinely meaningful to me was when I first *experienced* the Dharma, when I crossed the line from a reading Buddhist to a practicing Buddhist. Here was something that worked and was telling me to get up and experience my faith, rather than to listen to someone expound the fine points or read a holy scripture. I was supposed to find out on my own.

While beginning to meditate, I also realized that my brain needed help to get control of itself, which is provided in the form of medication prescribed by my psychiatrist. Once I had given my brain what it physically needed to provide for itself on a chemical level, I found I could practice meditation.

Months passed and everything was wonderful. My meditation practice was reaching beyond just plain sitting meditation. I began seeing the world though new and vibrant eyes. Optimism returned and with it a leveling out of my previous ups and downs. Quickly, though, another need became apparent, a need that had to be addressed in order for me to continue with my newfound sense of serenity.

Up to that point the Buddha and Dharma had been influential in my taking control of my own life. But I needed Sangha. Indiana has several prominent *sanghas* yet all of them are a number of hours away, and with a schedule like most other suburban teens in America, a six-hour round-trip drive to a monastery is just not practical. I needed something more than what a monastic community could provide for me; I needed other teens. Teens, people like me, facing the same problems that I was. Don't get me wrong, adults were and still are essential to my growth in the Dharma, but nothing is as fulfilling as having a group of peers understand your experiences not through distant recollection, but rather through their own present experiences.

My search began, but there was literally nothing. Every now and then I would find a web page, but none capable of providing what I needed and wanted. It seemed to me as if the younger Buddhists had been forgotten from the collective awareness of Dharma in the West, and were doing little to make themselves heard and known.

Everywhere I went teen Buddhists were nothing but a footnote. After a couple weeks of fruitless searches I decided I had to do something myself. That's when I first thought of the idea of TBS or *Teen Buddhist Sangha.*

Its medium would be the Internet, since it's something my generation has become so adept at communicating with. The members would be teens who were living the Dharma in their own lives and facing similar travails. The idea was that together we could persevere with a combined strength through the difficulties that come with adapting Buddhism to the Western world and our daily lives. The sangha would break ground as being the first to specifically target the teen age bracket, incorporating instant messaging, email listservs, and a web page. With this idea I took flight, and from hours of work by myself and others who first joined over two and a half years ago, TBS became a sangha in the truest sense of its definition. TBS became a working, living, collective entity, standing witness to the ability of the Dharma to adapt to and thrive in any type of environment. My final piece of the Triple Gem was in place.

Founding TBS sent my confidence soaring. I now had regular contact with an entire spectrum of people just like me who were keystrokes away and willing to listen, relate, and learn from one another. With time my sighs grew less and less deep, while my breaths of meditation deepened exponentially.

These days depression is still part of my life, but is no longer a defining characteristic. It's not easy. Before, suffering is what seemed to rob my life of its meaning, whereas now the Dharma has helped me to see that suffering is what actually *provides* life its meaning. Now, whenever I feel the ground start to dip below my feet and I know that another "down session" is on its way, I take a deep breath, hold it, and then release it—*without* a sigh.

Buddhism Is My Constant

Tenzin Youdon Takshamtsang

Growing up in a Tibetan community in northern India, I was taught Buddhist values, like respecting teachers and not harming other sentient beings, in a simple way from my family and Tibetan culture. I first learned about Buddhism by watching my grandparents perform their daily rituals. They woke up early in the morning to chant at the family altar, where they kept a statue of the Buddha, carvings of other deities, and scriptures. They made offerings by burning incense, serving tea, pouring water, and lighting butter lamps. We took refuge in the precious jewels by chanting *"Lama la khapso cheyo, Sangye la khapso cheyo, Choe la khapso cheyo, Gyenduen la khapso cheyo"* ("I take refuge in the Guru, I take refuge in the Buddha, I take refuge in the Dharma, I take refuge in the Sangha"). Then we prostrated three times in front of the family altar, bringing our foreheads to the seat of the offerings. Throughout the rest of the day, there were other rituals to remind me of Buddhism. Before eating meals, my grandparents would offer the first piece of the best food to the altar and recite prayers. We would prostrate three times on our bed before going to sleep.

Tenzin Youdon Takshamtsang, 19, is the founder of a Students for a Free Tibet chapter at her school, Lesley College, and a member of the Buddhist community.

Often, my grandmother and I went to the nearby monastery to circumambulate the temple grounds. She carried a rosary in her hand, whispering *mantras*. The mantra *om mani padme hung,* the six sacred syllables that represent the six realms of life, is written on my tongue ever since I can remember. The monastery was also a meeting place, so we would spend time with others we knew there. My grandmother took me to the monastery for blessings whenever I was ill or even when I had bad dreams. Although I used to think that life with my grandparents was boring, I realize now that it was boring in a very interesting way. In fact, it would be better to think of it as simple, rather than boring.

My parents taught me the Buddhist principle of treating everybody equally no matter what race or caste. They also taught me the importance of helping others. I have learned that happiness is the main purpose of our life and, whatever we do, we do it for our happiness. Through my parents I realized that happiness comes from your inner mind, being content with what you have and being happy with who you are. My parents taught me that all Buddhists seek liberation, or inner freedom, and that everyone has the potential to gain this enlightenment as a *bodhisattva*. Tibetan Buddhists also believe in the law of *karma,* the universal law of cause and effect. Whatever I do today will bear fruit tomorrow, which implies that what I have done in the past created who I am today.

I also have learned about reincarnation because in my family there are two reincarnated *lamas,* or learned masters. My uncle Taksham is the seventh reincarnation of Taksham Nueden Dorjee of the Nyingma lineage. My cousin Shewalha is a reincarnated lama recognized when he was three years old by His Holiness the Fourteenth Dalai Lama. When I was younger, I felt a little jealous when my cousin, who is only two years older, got so much attention from people coming to get blessings from him and to offer cash and gifts to him. To me, he was just a normal kid who was naughty, but to others he was a special kid, a reincarnation of Shantideva, who wrote the famous book *The Bodhisattva's Way of Life*. Today, my cousin is twenty-three and studies as a monk at Sera Monastery in South India. From a young age, I was taught how essential lamas are in our religion and was shown how to behave in the presence of a lama.

When I was nine years old, I was sent to a Tibetan boarding school in Dharamsala, Northern India, where Buddhist teachings were strictly followed. We had special Buddhist instructors and a small temple, where I was taught Buddhist scriptures and prayers. All the Tibetan students congregated in the school hall and recited prayers for at least an hour every night. We observed religious days in the school. My friends and I prayed hard, especially during annual examinations, with the belief that the prayers would bring the best of luck. After reading a prayer book, we raised the sacred text to our forehead out of respect and for even greater blessings. During our school's three-month winter vacation, we would visit a Tibetan settlement where my father was working. There again I was steeped in a world full of Buddhist activities. Everyone carried *malas* (rosaries) while the chanting of monks in their monasteries floated out into the streets.

During winter break, I also had the opportunity to make pilgrimages to holy places like Varanasi for Kalachakra teachings. I will never forget my visit during *monlam*, a month-long religious festival, to Bodhgaya—the place where Lord Buddha attained enlightenment. There were hundreds of beggars near the holy sites who brought the oldest and most crippled members of their family with them as a way of drawing sympathy out for their family's suffering. I brought tons of coins to give out, but even that wasn't enough. There were also peddlers who wanted to sell fish to us so that we could free them in the holy pond, but I found it pointless because they caught the fish from the same pond. Although it was a clever business, I paid for the fish's release because at least I could help the poor peddler. From these travels, I am constantly reminded to treat everybody equally with love and compassion.

Even though I did not think about it at the time, now that I am older I realize that these experiences have influenced my understanding of who I am and what I want to become. Something as simple as the heritage of my name shapes me: Tenzin Youdon was given to me by His Holiness the Dalai Lama. *Tenzin,* meaning "holder of the teachings," is part of the Dalai Lama's name, and *Youdon* is "Green Tara."

I came to the United States when I was fifteen. In America, it is harder for me to do daily prayers like I used to in my school in India. We have a modest altar in our home where we keep statues of Lord Buddha and other deities. The altar also has a prominent portrait of His Holiness the Dalai Lama, who I consider a genuine manifestation of the Lord of Compassion and who is my root master, with whom I take refuge whenever life becomes chaotic. Our living room looks like a shrine, with displays of *thangkas,* hanging scrolls of Buddhist images. In our busy, modern lives, we hardly have time to change the daily offerings and chant or read scriptures. So, these Buddhist images and altar have become more like decorations. Still, like my family, other Tibetans in America are trying hard to preserve our culture, religion, and traditional way of life—although monthly bills always chase them. Sometimes it seems like the Tibetans who've come to America are more concerned with earning money, getting a better house and car, and going on vacation. The young Tibetans my age are often focused on their studies so that they can earn a degree to get a high-paying job. We aren't as steeped in Buddhist studies and practices as we were in India, but we are also missing the Buddhist culture that engulfed us so it's harder to sustain what we had in India, too. Nonetheless, I consider myself a Buddhist because Buddhism, in a basic way, means being kind and honest, respecting elders, forgiving others, and believing in rebirth and karma. I believe that to be a Buddhist one doesn't have to be in a monastery or be a strict practitioner. Today, I make an effort to attend Buddhist festivals, receive teachings by visiting lamas, and take part in the Buddhist community at my college. I am learning the Buddhist teaching that life is always changing as I navigate my way through three identities: I have my own Tibetan culture, the years I grew up in the rich culture of India, and now my life as an American. But Buddhism is my constant.

Twenties and Thirties

PRACTICE

Nothing Special

SUMANA BHIKKHU (JAKE H. DAVIS)

Just after graduating high school, I spent the better part of a year traveling in Asia, ending my trip with a three-week meditation retreat at the Kyaswa Monastery in the Sagaing Hills of Upper Burma. I felt an immediate familiarity with the Burmese language and customs and the simple way of life practiced by the monks and nuns. It felt like I was returning home, and I knew I would be back.

A few years later, I found myself again in Burma, sitting on a bright-green carpet in the meditation hall of Kyaswa Monastery. A painted Buddha figure with a flashing halo of colored LED lights was at the front. The abbot with whom I had practiced on my first visit, Sayadaw U Lakkhana, sat below the altar. He held a set of gold-painted rectangular wooden tablets inscribed with the Pali text for ordination. When the ceremony was finished, I was told to think of my preceptor as a father, to follow the monks' *Vinaya* rules—the monastic code of conduct—with care and diligence, and to remember the current date and time so that I would always know which monks I was senior or junior to,

Sumana Bhikkhu (Jake H. Davis), 24, is a monk in the Theravada lineage of Sayadaw U Pandita.

even by a minute. With my palms pressed together at my chest in the traditional gesture of respect, I received ordination as a *bhikkhu*, a monk.

In Theravada Buddhism, women and men can ordain for as long as they are willing to maintain the full discipline, from a few days to an entire lifetime. Many young people all over Burma and Southeast Asia spend some time as a temporary nun or monk. Living as a *bhikkhu* was a powerful rite of passage for me, as well. The outer transformation included a new name: U Sumanasiri, meaning something like "one with the glory of a good mind." It included new appearance: a shaved head and ochre robes. It included, most importantly, a new way of living: gathering alms from lay supporters and observing the discipline of a celibate mendicant. I fantasized also of a inner transformation, and in due time this too came, though it was much more challenging than I had imagined.

A few weeks after my ordination, I went to see the renowned meditation master Sayadaw U Pandita. My first mentors in the practice, Steven Smith and Michele McDonald, are devoted students of U Pandita's, and I had heard a great deal about him. I was in awe sitting there in front of him in that first evening, my still unfamiliar robes damp with sweat and falling down around me. After inquiring about my intentions in studying Burmese and Pali, U Pandita accepted me as a student and sent me to study with one of his senior monks at a forest monastery nearby.

I was unusual among Westeren visitors to Burma in that I could speak some Burmese, which I had studied at Marlboro College in Vermont. I soon settled into a routine of studying and helping with the interpretation needs of foreign meditators. As my Burmese became increasingly fluent, I was given more responsibility around the monastery. In addition to taking care of foreign meditators, I translated a biography of U Pandita into

English, gave an hour-long talk in Burmese, and tried to inspire a number of local people to come meditate. Though I had originally intended to stay only six months, I grew more and more enchanted by the idea of spending the rest of my years as a monk. I felt intoxicated with the amount of approval and encouragement I was getting. I did my best to impress my teachers and hoped desperately that Sayadaw U Pandita was taking notice.

After nearly eight months of study and work, I went into a long meditation retreat, which included interviews with the teacher. I had become fluent enough in Burmese to make my reports directly, and I asked special permission to have interviews with U Pandita himself. He gave me a great deal of time and care, and after a few months of retreat, I felt my energy soar and my confidence rise. Then, unexpectedly, Sayadaw shifted into a seemingly more aggressive mode in the interviews.

Every evening I would enter his room timidly, bow, and hold my palms together. I would then report to him a few of my recent experiences in meditation practice: sensations of the breath, of walking, and so on. Each time, when I was done reporting he would ask with a disappointed expression, "Is that all?"

"That's all, Venerable Sir," I would reply, a sinking feeling growing in my chest.

"It's nothing special," he would say. Repeated day after day, this routine became increasingly frustrating. What was I missing?

One evening, exasperated, I tried reporting a few more things, some interesting emotional and visual experiences.

"Nothing special at all," Sayadaw said curtly, and turned to other business.

I walked out of the interview with my head spinning. This word the teacher had used, *htu,* was confusing; it could mean "special," but also "extraordinary," "weird," or just "different." Perhaps there was some meaning of the word *htu* that I was missing. Maybe that is why I seemed unable to give Sayadaw what he was looking for. Especially in moments of frustration, I began to doubt myself: my understanding of Burmese, my ability to practice meditation, my dreams of training with U Pandita.

I spent that night and the following day worrying about what "special" experience I was failing to attain. Though I tried to set these thoughts aside and concentrate on my breath, after a few hours I would find myself stuck again in these incessant worries. I soon became terrified that I was losing my concentration, and with it all my dreams of myself as a "successful" monk. Without concentration, there would be no progress in my meditation, I was sure, and Sayadaw would surely want nothing do to with someone who was a such failure. This, too, was a very scary train of thought, impossible to break out of, and no doubt deadly to my ability to practice, I told myself coldly. Over the next month fear built upon fear, sending me into an emotional tailspin.

I came out of that retreat very shaken. Though I spent three more months in Burma doing interpretation for interviews, I spent these last months feeling broken and lost. I was torn between staying with U Pandita and returning home, too terrified to take any new course, too ashamed to stay where I was.

U Pandita forced me to navigate this storm for myself. One morning just before I finally decided to leave, I reported how mind-states of self-judgment and doubt were overwhelming me. Sayadaw gave me a curt reply in Burmese:

"Of course that would be true if you didn't know how to be mindful," he said.

Sayadaw's reply surprised me. Thinking that perhaps I had misunderstood, I timidly asked him to repeat himself.

"Of course that would be true if you didn't know how to be mindful," he said again. Then he got up, walked out of the room, and shut the door with a resounding thud.

I was stung by Sayadaw's brusque tone. After a year studying and practicing at his monastery, I had come to enjoy the fact that U Pandita took a special interest in my studies, granting me opportunities usually reserved for longtime students. He clearly appreciated my ability to speak Burmese. He often checked to make sure that my accommodations and food were satisfactory, and he had given me a set of the special Malaysian robes he normally reserved for monks working at the center. When he slammed his door that morning, it shook me deeply.

Still feeling ambivalent, I finally left Burma and the ordained life a few days after that encounter. I had stayed there, living as a monk, for fifteen months. I returned the following year, this time with my mentor, Steven, and a good deal of trepidation. When we went to pay respects to U Pandita, however, he beamed at me and joked in Burmese, inquiring about my studies and how I had been since he last saw me.

The year following that brief trip back I spent finishing my college studies as well as slowly rebuilding my self-confidence; by the next spring I felt ready to return to Burma for six-weeks of practice. It had been over two years since I had practiced as a monk with U Pandita. This time, more wary of getting caught in dreams of future glory, I found a new ease in the simplicity of focusing on present experience.

A few months later, Sayadaw came to teach a retreat in the U.S., and I volunteered to assist. In addition to translating for interviews, I became Sayadaw's masseur. Each evening, as I worked on loosening his eighty-year-old muscles, Sayadaw lay on his back querying me about my family, the Bible, American history and culture, and the American meditation community, dropping gems of wisdom along the way. "I'm learning a lot from you," Sayadaw would say at the end each evening, using an affectionate Burmese term of direct address.

In reflecting on my relationship with Sayadaw U Pandita, I have come to realize that he loved me in the purest way: because he truly wanted my welfare and happiness, he was not afraid to force me to face my deepest fears. Sayadaw saw how attached I was to praise, how desperately I wanted to be special. When I practiced with him, I came to see for myself how much suffering this pattern was causing me. Though that year as a monk was one of the most painful periods of my life, I have come to see it as one of the most valuable.

Fortune Baby?

ALEXIS TRASS

In my tradition of Nichiren Buddhism, people born into this practice are sometimes called fortune babies. But when I was a kid, I wasn't so sure that I was all that fortunate to be Buddhist while growing up in the Christian culture of Gary, Indiana.

My parents were Buddhist converts who began practicing Buddhism two years before I was born. My mother would often say how she wished she had known about Buddhism when she was my age and how I was so lucky to be born into the practice.

I didn't feel lucky at all and I secretly wished my parents would start going back to church.

When I was about five years old, I began to get the impression that I was different from my peers because I didn't believe in God. I remember in kindergarten that every afternoon we had a snack of milk and cookies. Before eating, the teacher would lead the class in saying grace. Even though it was 1980, it was still a time when mandates to separate church and state were largely ignored in my community. I still remember the simple prayer:

Alexis Trass, 27, a lifelong practitioner of Nichiren Buddhism, is the associate editor of Living Buddhism *magazine, a monthly journal for the Soka Gakkai International-USA.*

God is great
God is good
Let us thank Him
For our food

It didn't occur to me that I wasn't supposed to say grace or that it ran counter to what my parents were teaching me at home about religion. When I mentioned the prayer casually to them one day, they exchanged looks that I didn't understand. They asked me questions and I told them about it. My father told me not to say grace anymore. The next day, he went to the school, told the teacher that my family was Buddhist, and that I would no longer be joining them in grace. So, for the few moments that my classmates bowed their hands, palms pressed together to thank God for their food, I sat upright and silent. Some kids asked why I wasn't saying grace anymore. My answer was that I didn't know; at five years old I didn't really understand religious differences.

It would be an understatement to say that it was *difficult* for me to tell my friends and classmates that I was a Buddhist—it was downright impossible. Whenever I mentioned it to someone, I would inevitably get a wide-eyed look of disbelief or, worse, disapproval. As much as I didn't want to tell people about my family's religious beliefs, it was sometimes unavoidable. When friends came over, they wanted to know what that big box was in the living room. "Is that a cabinet?" they would ask. (The cabinet is really the altar where we kept a long scroll with the title of the Lotus Sutra brushed in classical Chinese characters.) When I was on the phone, they wanted to know what that bell-ringing noise was in the background. "Uhhh . . . that's just the doorbell," I would say. Never mind that we didn't have a doorbell. (During recitation of the *sutra*, practitioners ring a bell after each prayer, as is the tradition.)

But it wasn't just at home I encountered these problems. Once at school, an argument about who had the best peanut butter and jelly sandwich quickly escalated into a personal attack about why I didn't go to church. It was no use trying to explain. By and large, people where I grew up were Christian, or at least believed in God, and their thinking was just narrow enough to believe that everybody else must be Christian as well. I was sometimes treated as a freak of nature. Insults were tossed my way or my schoolmates would stay away from me for fear of being struck down by God because of their association with me.

I grew to be ashamed of being a Buddhist. It seemed more trouble than it was worth for someone who desperately desired—for even one day—to be like everybody else.

But there was another world I could visit, a place where I belonged and where it was a good thing to be a Buddhist. The Nichiren Buddhists in my area had organized a vibrant youth group that had tons of fun activities. For instance, when I turned eleven, I joined the Nichiren youth group's fife and drum corps. With them, I traveled to New York, New Orleans, Philadelphia, and Minneapolis performing in parades and festivals. I even performed with others at Madison Square Garden!

Outside of public school and my friends, I liked my Buddhist practice. It was even fun for me to learn about certain Buddhist concepts like the oneness of life and the environment and the three thousand realms that exist in a single moment.

As a teenager, I began meeting people that really didn't care that I was a Buddhist. Still, I didn't feel confident enough to volunteer that information without a compelling reason. When I was fifteen, I got my first real boyfriend, whom I'll call Terry. I thought it was best I didn't mention Buddhism to him. Terry would come over to my house often since I wasn't allowed to actually go *out* on a date yet. He asked about our cabinet, the altar, a couple of times but I just brushed him off. One day when Terry was over, I could see my father preparing to do his evening prayers. He was dusting the altar and removing the water-offering cup. With all my might, I was mentally willing him to stop, to wait until Terry had left. Terry was putting on his coat right now, after all. But my father was not shy about anything, certainly not about praying in his own home.

I was rushing Terry to the door. He was taking his time talking to my mother and my sisters. I pulled his arm. My father was sitting down at the altar. I finally got Terry to the threshold. My father started ringing the bell. Terry turned around, his mouth dropped open and his eyes got bigger than humanly possible. No point in rushing now.

When we stepped outside, he asked what my father was doing. I told him that he was chanting *Nam-myoho-renge-kyo* and that we were Buddhist. After he got over the shock of seeing something so strange to him, Terry said he was upset that in the six months we had been going together, I never mentioned something so important. He said he didn't care what religion I practiced—he liked me for who I was. I was comforted by what he said, but not comforted enough to make me stick with Buddhism.

When I went to college, it was easy to not tell anybody about it. My parents weren't around to remind me to do my morning and evening prayers. Nobody could make me practice. I prayed only a little, and only during times of crisis. I started to think of Buddhism as something my parents did and by virtue of being born to them, something I had to do. I figured it was about time that I decided for myself what I would and would not practice. It was easy to let Buddhism fall by the wayside.

I wandered through my years in college thinking I was happy with my decision. When I graduated and had to join the "real world" I saw that my problems weren't easily solved and that I needed *something* to make me happy. My parents suggested that I really try practicing Buddhism for myself. Naturally I resisted.

After college graduation, I lived with my parents and taught junior high locally. My father volunteered me for a Buddhist youth activity without my knowledge. I felt obligated to be there since he told the organizers I would be. I went reluctantly, but during the course of the meeting I experienced an internal shift: I was happy. I became part of a committee working with young people, and as a schoolteacher I felt such great joy at the prospect of positively shaping the lives of those youth.

I was inspired to begin to practice Buddhism independently of my parents and I fell in love with it. For the first time in my life I felt free and powerful. We believe when there is a change in the depths of a person's life, that change is reflected in the whole person—in all of his or her component functions, activities, and relationships—and in the surrounding environment.

Practicing wholeheartedly, I felt—I deeply felt—that I could shape the course of my life. This is not to say that my life is always rosy. But I have a tool that allows me to bring forth my Buddha wisdom in every aspect of my life and make breakthroughs. It is a way of life for me that I will never let go of again.

Sometimes I'll meet other members of my organization who will say, "You're so lucky to be a fortune baby." That's simply not true—I'm no luckier than anybody else. But I smile because I *was* fortunate for many years and just didn't know it.

Home-Leaving and Home-Making

MYOJU MEG LEVIE

"What I need is a church."

That's what I thought after a five-year relationship had finally ended. I was twenty-four, feeling depressed and knew something needed to change. So I went church shopping, and I ended up at the Berkeley Zen Center. I felt immediately that it was a kind of homecoming for me.

Now, eleven years later, I am planning to ordain in the Japanese Soto Zen tradition. I also am married and have a one-year-old daughter. In most of the Buddhist world, family life and ordination remain mutually exclusive. Yet in Japanese Zen, largely through an accident of history, most priests—at least male ones—do marry and have families. But my path to this place was complex.

Very shortly after I began practicing with this community, a resolve to devote myself to Dharma practice rose up inside me, and I felt that the best way to do that was to stay single, ordain, and live as a celibate monastic.

Yet I had always been drawn to relationships, and I had always wanted children. I grew up with a particularly strong and loving

Myoju Meg Levie, 35, lives with her family at Green Gulch Farm Zen Center.

connection to my own mother and grandmother and had very positive associations with the role of motherhood.

After six months of intensive meditation practice, I met Jeremy. He arrived at the Zen Center with his own firm resolve to devote himself to practice. Soon after he arrived, he noticed, as I had, the strong partnerships that had developed there. Married couples who were longtime practitioners seemed to have remarkable relationships. Occasionally in public ceremonies where verbal exchange occurred, couples found themselves questioning each other face-to-face, and their words pointed to an unusual and lively intimacy.

Yet when Jeremy and I started a relationship, I felt intense internal conflict. I wanted to commit myself to practice through the public affirmation of ordination, and I feared that if we got married, so much would follow. I suspected I would change internally. I would want a family, and probably a house, and I might even forget the strong connection to practice that I felt.

Yet around us we had examples of lives in which ordination and family were not exclusive. Shunryu Suzuki-roshi, the Japanese teacher who founded the San Francisco Zen Center, was married and had four children. Our own teacher, Tenshin Reb Anderson, had raised a child at Zen Center, as had numerous other ordained people. As a way to address the tension between the demands of training as a priest and the demands of relationships and family, our teacher presented us with his own solution: that we should be Zen Center residents and not take on any new major commitments for five years after ordination. Jeremy and I could get married and then ordain, but he suggested we wait five years before having children. Or, we could choose not to ordain and go ahead, as any lay couple could, with starting a family. At thirty-three, I found myself wanting to ordain now and also not wait five years to have a child. Maybe it could all work, but the timing was very tight. Many women have children in their late thirties, but not all women can. Waiting until I was thirty-eight meant accepting that I might not have children at all, a thought that went against the grain of much of what I knew about myself. I remembered that when I had first started practicing Buddhism I had met a Taiwanese Zen master who had talked with me kindly about the choices of a traditional ordination and family. "Don't go too much against your own *karma*," he advised. "It's not good."

Jeremy and I married at Green Gulch Farm. We both planned to receive ordination the following April, accepting the five-year restriction. Though I didn't feel settled with the situation, I tried to convince myself, and everyone around me, that I did. A number of new families were living at Green Gulch, and I just could not stay around the babies—it was too painful. We decided to move back to Tassajara, where we hoped to feel more supported by living with people following a monastic schedule.

Not long after we returned to Tassajara, as the date of ordination approached, I decided to cut my hair very short. A few years earlier, I had gotten a buzz cut in preparation for lay ordination at the end of my first practice period at Tassajara. I remembered a settledness and joy in that symbolic surrender, but this time when I cut my hair something felt wrong. Entering the dining room one evening with newly-shorn hair, I found myself bumping into things and unable to look people in the eye. I also became aware of anger. Cutting my hair started to feel like a violent act.

I brought up my concerns with my teacher. He encouraged me to go ahead and have a baby instead of ordaining, if that's what I really wanted to do. I simply didn't want to hear that, since it wasn't clear when ordination would be possible if I did have a child. I felt Jeremy respected my wish to ordain while being concerned about waiting to have a child and the conflict I felt. Finally, two months before the ordination date, on a cool February morning at Tassajara, I was able to be completely honest with myself and my teacher. I realized that I was doing violence to myself internally by pushing down something so powerful, and that I was splitting myself in two. My teacher and I agreed that I would not ordain.

After leaving the interview room, I walked in my black sitting robes down to the end of the valley to the place where the path meets the creek. The winter rains had come and soaked the mountains. Now the creek ran full and wild. As soon as I got to the water's edge, I remembered: just before receiving lay ordination five years before, I had come to this same spot to lay my hair in the running water as an offering. Now after walking away from a second ordination, I had come to the creek to grieve. With everyone far away in the *zendo,* and the voice of the water louder than my own, I cried, I wailed, I let my heart break. In the midst of that release, I felt a clear, calm awareness, a feeling of deep liberation and happiness. I realized that although I had thought I had been clinging to a fantasy of having children, in fact I had been clinging to a fantasy of ordination.

Suddenly my relationship with formal practice shifted. From the beginning I had loved the traditional Japanese forms: the black sitting robes, the bowing and chanting, the precise way of moving in the zendo, and the silence. Now I could hardly stand to wear robes at all. In the summer at Tassajara, lay sitting robes are optional for zendo events. I would put on my robes in our cabin and then immediately take them off again, opting for dark pants and a shirt instead. They no longer seemed to fit me. I also had trouble staying for the liturgical service after meditation. All of what I had loved before—the formality, the Japanese-style chanting, the full prostrations—now seemed restrictive and foreign, and I slipped away whenever I could. I chafed at the silence and wanted to break out of it. Yet throughout, zazen did remain a refuge. During this time I was able to drop all of my ideas about ordained practice and discover what remained true for me: the intimate experience of meditation and the basic teachings of Buddhism. I felt great affirmation in my practice, and later when I could return to the forms, I found I was able to hold them more lightly.

At the end of the summer, we left Tassajara and moved into an apartment at City Center in San Francisco. Our daughter, Elizabeth, was born at home.

When I decided not to ordain, I gave it up completely and I didn't know if the opportunity would ever reappear in my life. I knew that if it did, it would be a different ordination because the circumstances of my life would be so different. Since having a child requires the commitment of both parents, and to avoid a conflict between the needs of a new baby and the demands of priest training, Jeremy also agreed not to ordain.

Just before Elizabeth turned one year old, I went to see a teacher who had himself raised a family at Zen Center. I hadn't gone to talk about ordination, and what came out of my mouth surprised me. "If I don't ordain," I asked him, "what will become of me? Will I always have this feeling that I somehow missed the boat?" "You might," he said. "If one has a strong inclination to a religious life, which you do, and you don't give it expression, you might feel that way."

A few months later, Jeremy, Elizabeth, and I went to Green Gulch for a seven-day silent retreat led by Tenshin-roshi. Jeremy and I shared a seat: one of us would sit the afternoon all the way through lunch the next day while one stayed with Elizabeth, and then we would trade. Jeremy and I talked to each other some on breaks, and at one point he made this offer: if I wanted to go ahead and ordain, he would support me. He would take care of Elizabeth in the mornings so I could make it to the zendo. As for his own ordination, he said he could wait.

When the wish to ordain resurfaced, I still had some questions regarding the discrepancy between traditional monastic ordination and ordination for people with families. If I did ordain, I would not be a nun or a "monastic" as I understood the terms. What would it mean to participate in a "home-leaving" ceremony and shave my head, at least temporarily, yet be a married woman with a child? Would an understanding of renunciation in a more abstract sense be sufficient? Although I still held these questions, such a strong inner request to ordain, whatever that meant, arose inside me that I realized I was willing to live with the contradictions. Regarding ordination, I asked myself, "Do I think this will be helpful and not harmful?" and the answer came back "Yes." I took the proposal that I would ordain with Jeremy's support to our teacher, who, after some consideration, agreed.

Traditional ordination has provided an opportunity for those seeking liberation to step outside the often exhausting demands of everyday labor and receive support to pursue the path of awakening. Living the renunciate life of a monk or nun discourages emotional entanglement and attachment, and personal needs remain simple. The advantages of such a life are numerous, and the Sangha has been a vehicle for the continuation of Buddhism for over two thousand years.

Yet when I look at the circumstances of my own life, I find an unusual degree of flexibility. Especially living in a Dharma center, I often experience a seamlessness in following a religious vocation and caring for a family. While I do not live the life of a traditional renunciate, I find constant reminders that there is nothing to hold onto, even here. I also draw encouragement from the thought that other religious traditions, such as Judaism and Protestant Christianity, have found use for people who are both ordained and have families, and I believe that Buddhism can as well.

Yet I also am aware of a loss. I can understand now in a way that I could not before what my teacher was trying to tell me: that children do change your life, that there is no going back, and some opportunities are lost. My practice has changed. I haven't followed the formal practice schedule regularly since my daughter was born, though I have maintained a sitting practice, and as she gets older I'm able to participate more in the schedule. My time is rarely my own, and I'm not as free to move around as I was before. But I remember appreciating a similar situation: monks in a monastery, they say, are like rocks in a tumbler, bumping into each other and wearing off each other's rough edges. There's no escape from such intimacy in home life, either.

Siddhartha Gautama left his sleeping wife and child to pursue his spiritual quest, and he never returned to domestic life. When I slip out of bed in the dark each morning to go to the zendo, leaving my husband and daughter, I feel I am reenacting his departure. Yet every morning I return.

The Dharma of Identity

Viveka Chen

I recently reread some of my early diaries, about my childhood in a nearly all-white, middle-class New Jersey suburb. The number of references to being called a "chink" was shocking. I had forgotten the frustration of being reduced to a hateful label. Memories swirled up in a complex cocktail of humiliation, sadness, and indignation: standing in the school yard listening to blonde, blue-eyed girls sing jump rope songs that mocked my "dried squid breath"; unwittingly reading my best friend's diary entry confessing embarrassment at being seen with a horde of Chinese on a ski trip; and hearing the ignorant slurs casually dropped in the lunch room. I remembered my superficial coping mechanisms, like wearing a clothespin on my nose to make it thinner, begging my mom for meat loaf, and insisting on speaking to my parents in English, even when they spoke to me in Chinese. I didn't know how to love myself because the world around me didn't know how to love me either.

My first trip to China to visit family at the age of sixteen saved me from identity oblivion. On that trip, I experienced China's rich

Viveka Chen, 34, a second-generation Chinese American ordained in the Western Buddhist Order, is working to make meditation accessible to people of color and activists.

history and culture. My aunts and cousins, like countless others, had survived the punishments of the Cultural Revolution, including hard manual labor and years of moving bricks and shoveling manure. Yet, people were warm hearted and full of life. Somehow I was connected to all of this. The Yellow Mountains at sunrise, the Great Wall, Buddhist temples, roadside red bean popsicle vendors, and over a billion people. *Chinese* people! It felt as if I had forgotten what it was to be Chinese and returning woke me up from an identity coma. For a girl who grew up as only one of two Chinese people in her American school, it was a huge shift in perspective. After that trip, I began the process of letting go of the self-loathing I had absorbed.

A few years later, in college, I set about purposely addressing my ethnic amnesia. I immersed myself in Chinese history, political science, and language, stumbling across Buddhism in a Chinese philosophy course. Reading my first Dharma book, I was again overtaken by a sense of remembering, as if I had long been a Buddhist. Although my very traditional grandmother was a Buddhist, she never inspired me. As children, my brother and I hid behind the couch and mimicked her chanting, cracking ourselves up in laughter. Not an auspicious start to the Path! Yet, while Grandmother's devotions did not impress me, I did respond to the *ideas* of Buddhism, especially an outlook that transcended duality. After all, I myself was neither East nor West, and was also both.

I realized at some point that I could not simply read about Buddhism and that my self-directed practice had reached a limit. Travel in Buddhist Asian countries provided a glimpse of the depth of the tradition, but those foreign cultural forms felt unnatural and I hoped to find a place that reflected my own cultural context. The Buddhist path took off when, by luck, a free paper pointed me to a meditation class put on by the Friends of the

Western Buddhist Order. The FWBO offered the Buddhist tradition, still rigorous, still radical, but translated into a contemporary expression. Through an FWBO center in San Francisco, I found a place to learn meditation and practice Buddhism.

I appreciated that the Order was founded on the conviction that the essence of Buddhism is not limited to any particular cultural expression. Yet, I found few people of color at the Center. The culture at the Center, based on the principles of wisdom and compassion, was inspiring and even a lifeline for me. But I sometimes found the lack of diversity and multi-cultural perspective stifling or simply tiring.

A simple but ongoing example of the challenge came up when, at some point, I made an effort to create *sangha,* or spiritual community. Over the years Western women have been confused and even threatened by my seeming reservation and hesitation to share myself with them. I was aware that Western friendships are often built on the reciprocal exchange of problems and support, but I am very Chinese in this regard. My ordination name reflects my character: *Viveka* means "detachment" and refers to the solitude of meditation. In trying to create meaningful connections with my Dharma sisters, the complexity of achieving this while also being genuinely myself can be disheartening. I face painful flashbacks to that childhood feeling of not being loved as I am and an external pressure to be what I'm not—white.

Still, I have committed myself to staying with the FWBO over the years. For myself, the drive to seek out and practice the Dharma always outweighed the obvious lack of diversity around me in the "Western" forms of Buddhism, comprised predominately of white converts. I simply wasn't to be dissuaded from practice. The experience of being in-between cultures all my life has provided some resiliency. I also trust in the FWBO's values of cultural adaptation and inclusiveness, even if they were far from perfectly realized on the ground. Finally, I acknowledged that the Western tradition in which I practice and my predominantly Anglo teachers and peers in the sangha have provided much of the sustenance needed on my spiritual journey over the past thirteen years.

But on a broader scale, outside my community, I have seen and heard how the lack of diversity in sanghas creates a real and sometimes insurmountable barrier for those trying to get established on the Buddhist path. Once, a Chicano friend went on an Anglo-led retreat for activists of color. In the unfamiliar silence, he suddenly felt unwelcome and oppressed. He actually tried hiking out but it was too far to town to escape! In the end, he stayed and wrote a poem about his experience of being "Other." I find the closing line beautiful and healing. "I breathe in Buddha, I breathe out Mexican."

I continue to think about what can be done to make Buddhism more accessible and culturally appropriate to all those who seek the teachings. The limited diversity across the convert Buddhist traditions speaks to a challenge that I am trying to address in my leadership position at the FWBO center in San Francisco. We now hold regular people of color (POC) meditation gatherings and retreats. Thankfully, the sangha is gradually becoming more diverse.

Sometimes people of color want to leave behind "otherness" and *just be*. I do. That's one reason people of color settings can feel so nourishing. I benefit greatly from the sense of relaxation, shared struggle, and mutual encouragement. At the same time I continue to value the practice I am honored to share with the sangha at large. For me, much of what Buddhism is about is providing individual human beings with whatever will help them break through to wisdom and compassion and reveal their authentic self.

Recently, a Salvadoran youth shared his meditation experience saying that he had "contacted his indigenousness." The so-called original face of all beings, the face before your parents' face, is Buddha nature. It is unlimited, a completely open dimension of being, and ultimately ungraspable. Buddha nature is the potential for enlightenment that every human being possesses. Reflecting that we share this nature is recognition of our basic solidarity. It is to recognize the preciousness of human life across color lines.

Studying the Menu

ALAN G. WAGNER

I sit at a table in a small seminar room with seven or eight fellow students, all hunched over our copies of a Buddhist philosophical text in Chinese. Silence. I scratch my head. Someone coughs. Finally, our teacher speaks. "Well, if no one's got any better ideas, let's go on to the next sentence."

We typically get through about half a page of text in one three-hour session of a Buddhist Studies seminar—a whole page if we're really flying, but often only a few lines. We stop constantly to discuss background information, debate alternate readings, and quibble about punctuation. We've already spent hours working on the text at home, searching through dictionaries for obscure characters and looking up the quotations embedded within the text.

Doing scholarly research in Buddhism is a journey of thousands upon thousands of small steps. Rarely is there a flash of insight. Zen teachers sometimes say that learning about Buddhism is just reading a menu; practicing meditation is tasting the food. I haven't been able to separate the two: they've gone

Alan G. Wagner, 31, is a Ph.D. student at Harvard University, where he studies premodern Chinese Buddhism.

hand in hand for as long as I've been involved in the Dharma. Both have evolved in ways I wouldn't have expected.

When I arrived at graduate school seven years ago I had no intention of embarking on an academic career. My parents are both college professors, and I certainly was not going to follow in their footsteps. I was enrolled in a Master's degree program—two or three years to explore these cool Asian religions I had discovered after college, see if any of them made sense, get a diploma and then go *do* something. I figured I should also learn a difficult language while my brain was still young and flexible, and I vacillated between Chinese and Japanese. I settled on Chinese, reasoning that China was the up-and-coming nation of the future. Plus, I like Chinese food.

I took classes in Buddhism, and found myself confronted with ideas that made no sense to me, phrases such as "attachment to non-attachment" and "neither thinking nor non-thinking: without-thinking." I decided that I had to undertake some formal training in Buddhist practice in order to understand what these people were talking about. Otherwise, I would be like a blind man trying to understand red and blue.

Not that I started practicing meditation purely for academic reasons. I had tried *vipassana* before, though without much satisfaction. On the other hand something about the Zen path appeared simple and straightforward: *Just sit. See your own nature. Get enlightenment.* I didn't see any of the stuff here that I had rejected from my Catholic upbringing: the rituals, the intermediaries, the guilt, the blame. Still, I approached Zen practice with a certain amount of mistrust. I wasn't about to suspend my own critical judgment and blindly embrace whatever some authority told me. My academic work gave me a reason to try it out while still keeping a safe distance. At the same time, I felt seduced by the idea of enlightenment as a form of spiritual perfection that seemed reachable in a way that Catholic sainthood never had.

A few months after arriving in Cambridge, I went to a public appearance by Zen Master Seung Sahn at the Cambridge Zen Center. The Dharma hall was packed—standing room only—but I was lucky enough to have gotten a cushion on the floor. I looked around as the room got warmer and warmer, noticing that a Zen master attracts a much bigger crowd than a professor giving a lecture.

Seung Sahn taught by answering questions, and I wasn't shy about asking mine: "Should I become a monk?"

"Why would you do that?" he asked.

"To get enlightenment."

Seung Sahn grinned. "Enlightenment? You have a *big* problem!"

I was confused. Seung Sahn went on to explain what he meant. "If you have the mind to become a monk, you become a monk. If you have the mind to do something else, you do something else." The point is to get clear about who you are, without preconceived notions about who you should be.

The Zen tradition has lots of techniques to break through students' attachment to words and ideas, from Seung Sahn's jibes to phrases like "enlightenment is not different from delusion." In my academic training I was also learning the limits of words, learning how much of what we think we know about the world and about other people is really just a projection of ourselves.

I began to let go of my attachment to the word *enlightenment*. Gradually, I learned to stop wondering what enlightenment means and what it must be like. I've stopped setting up enlightenment now as a goal to be attained, and try to focus instead on my own actions and choices, in every situation and every moment. If someone asked me today what enlightenment is, I would have to say that honestly I don't know.

My understanding of practice has had to change. At first, I tried to keep my mind completely focused on my breath—without wavering for an instant, a single unbroken stream of breath-consciousness. After all, that's what I saw "on the menu." Zen texts describe the mind in meditation as being like a mirror, constantly reflecting what is present. But a funny thing happened. My vision would go dim, then black out completely with my eyes wide open. I could see again as soon as I directed my attention to my visual field. It was a little frightening and distracted me from staying with the breath.

My teacher said I was trying too hard. I was focusing so much on my breath that my mind stopped paying attention to my other senses. I tried to relax and just count the breaths, to stop striving for a particular mental state as I sat. Eventually I became able simply to notice my thoughts coming and going, and then I felt that I had started to understand something. I could watch remembered images arising from my past in exactly the same way that I could watch the sunlight falling on the wooden floor of the Dharma hall. I could listen to the stream of thoughts in my head—what psychologists call the inner monologue—in the same way that I could listen to the birds chirping outside. From this perspective there was no way to separate what was "inside" from what was "outside," no way to distinguish "me" from "not me."

Meditative practice takes discipline, as does academic work, and while I'm a student, the two do compete. For a couple of weeks at the start of each semester I would sit regularly every morning, and then as homework piled up I would start skipping days, doing unfinished work from the night before, until halfway through the term I was barely sitting at all. Early on, I asked a fellow student about this problem and he good-naturedly said something like, "Oh, yeah, that's how it is around here. You learn that there are times to practice really hard, and then there are times to just try to be mindful as you're walking to class." At that time I was still hooked on "getting enlightenment," and wasn't completely convinced that my friend knew what he was talking about, despite the fact that he had much more experience with Buddhism than I. Later I came to see that he was advising me to make a less rigid distinction between practice on a cushion and practice in everything I do in life.

Now I understand this non-distinction better, by rooting the idea of practice in the *bodhisattva*'s vow to save the numberless beings. This means that I am engaged in ongoing service to help others, a mission that will last endless lifetimes. If I see that what "I" am is not different from everything that is, then the choice I face becomes how best to use my own talents and gifts, to act in every moment for the benefit of those around me.

As it turns out, I don't have so much a monk's mind as I do a scholar's mind, an ability and natural inclination to investigate the ancient documents of the Buddhist tradition and to see what they might mean to us today in the light of critical evaluation. To me, this is a Buddhist practice, a way of serving others. I now wonder, could it be that the menu is not different from the food?

Crossing Over

JEFF WILSON

With the sharp clear ring of the bell, I settle onto my cushion. The *zendo* is calm as everyone prepares for meditation. Cheating, I take a look around at the group I'm visiting tonight: there are fifteen people gathered, backs straight, legs crossed, facing the wall. Dogen would be proud. It's inspiring to see something once so foreign to American religious life make the transition to an acceptable practice just short of the mainstream. This adaptability, genuine search, and enthusiasm are what I love about Zen in America.

But I notice other aspects that bother me. Though the majority of Buddhists in America are Asian, everyone in this zendo is of European descent. I'm the only one under thirty years old; most are in their forties and fifties. In the parking lot, my beat-up pickup truck stands out among the SUVs and imported cars. Unlike the churches, synagogues, mosques, or Hindu temples I've seen, there are no families.

In the silence of the zendo, my thoughts lead back to my early encounters with Buddhism. In college, I discovered how the

Jeff Wilson, 26, is a member of the New York Buddhist Church and is pursuing a Ph.D. in religious studies at the University of North Carolina.

concepts of emptiness, impermanence, and no-self resonated with my daily experience and worldview. I was impressed by Buddhism's emphasis on compassion for all beings and the peacefulness of its adherents.

Through the people I met and the books I read, I was presented with a certain model of what Buddhism is, or should be. Emerging Western or American Buddhism was said to be one superior to that found in Asia. The proponents of this new Buddhism often told me that I was lucky to be an American—I wasn't raised to believe in the extra stuff tacked on to Buddhism that distorted the Buddha's true message, a message of self-reliance, atheism, and anti-ritualism. Here in America we were uncovering the core of Buddha's teaching by stripping away the trappings. And the heart of this true Buddhism was intensive meditation practice, rather than chanting, prayers, bows, and the superstitious beliefs of "ethnic" Buddhism. That attitude informs the Zen meeting this evening. The walls are bare, our zafus are black, our clothing muted. There aren't any candles, statues, or incense. We recited moral precepts, but devotional prayers or chants are taboo.

The longer I practiced Zen, the more I encountered problems. Zen was making me more egotistical than before. I'd overplayed Zen's emphasis on self-power. Over several years I felt that rather than emptying the mind and realizing no-self, I was just swelling my head and making things worse for myself.

Ting! The bell sounds again. I've spent the whole period daydreaming. Everyone jumps up for walking meditation. Heads bowed, eyes averted, we slowly circumambulate the room. There's no socializing, even in this more active part of the meeting. I'm left to my own interior processes.

Back on the cushion, I recollect my pilgrimage to "the other side of Buddhism in America" that I began a few years ago. I had decided that, rather than accept the criticisms about other Buddhist sects I heard at the local zendo, I would actively seek out other communities that seemed so foreign to Buddhism as I understood it.

Over the course of months I attended traditional Theravadin *dana* ceremonies, went to concerts sponsored by Soka Gakkai, wore myself out from prostrations at Chinese Mahayana temples, and participated in Buddhist group therapy with Rissho Kosei-Kai. I read scriptures with Koreans, received holy water blessings from Ceylonese monks, discussed empowerments with Tibetans, and chanted *mantras* with the Vietnamese. Before long, I'd had my fortune read, released animals for merit, prayed to an East Asian war god, and had my *karma* purified by Japanese tantric monks. The sheer diversity and richness of Buddhist practice in America was mind-boggling.

As a Zennist I had especially looked down on the Pure Land traditions, which were also found in Japan, assuming they were shallow, quasi-theistic sects mired in blind faith and escapism. Yet, I had learned that most Japanese follow this form of Buddhism and that very few, including monastics, actually practice the meditation that I had thought was the sine qua non of Buddhism. I resisted visiting a Jodo Shinshu (the largest Japanese school of Pure Land) temple, but finally I decided that my pilgrimage would be incomplete if I didn't at least make one trip to such a group.

The worship hall of the New York Buddhist Church (part of the Jodo Shinshu tradition) seemed a lot like a Christian church. Rows of chairs led toward an altar space where a golden statue was enshrined. Offerings of fruit and rice sat before it, and candles and incense lent an air of other-worldliness to the semi-lit hall. The austerity of the Zen meditation hall seemed very far away, and caught in these unfamiliar surroundings, I wondered if that wasn't where I belonged after all. I was ready to leave when a loud bell sounded with a crash and the service began. Now there was no escape.

The congregation launched into a long chant, and at first the transliteration felt like marbles in my mouth. But as I caught on to the rhythm, it began to seem natural. My critical mind was left in the dust as I raced to keep up with the rest of the group, and the chanting began to make my chest and head vibrate. In the zendo I always had to be on guard against falling asleep, but here I was suddenly energized, fully present to the beauty and genuineness of the ceremony handed down over so many centuries. Glancing around, I saw an impressively integrated *sangha,* with Asian-Americans, European-Americans, and African-Americans. Men and women of all ages were joining in the chant. I realized that they'd gathered to express their joy and thankfulness at sharing in the Dharma. There was real spirit here, something I hadn't often encountered in the meditation-oriented groups.

After the chant, the minister gave a sermon in English, using stories from regular life to illustrate his points, instead of perplexing Zen *koans* or ancient *sutras.* He talked about the importance of kindness, of remembering our indebtedness to all things, and not thinking that Buddhist practice made us better than other people. Then he invited newcomers to stand up and introduce themselves. As each of us called out our names, the congregation smiled and clapped. I was surprised—I'd rarely been to a Buddhist group that actively embraced outsiders and where the focus was fully on the needs of ordinary people, rather than the charisma of the teacher, the correctness of the practice, or the proper performance of the ritual.

Afterward, everyone gathered to socialize and eat. Kids were running everywhere, women served tea and refreshments, and lots of folks came up to shake my hand. Many were lifelong Buddhists, while others were converts, and for once I encountered several other twenty-somethings at a Buddhist service. They all shared an infectious warmth, friendliness, and humility, and I felt glad to have swallowed my fears and prejudices to attend services that morning. Without really intending to make it a trend, I found myself at the temple again the next week, and the week after that.

Over time my preconceptions about Pure Land Buddhism were overcome, and the more I explored, the deeper I realized this path was. According to Jodo Shinshu (also known as Shin Buddhism), it's nearly impossible for us to transcend the self/non-self mentality—we're stuck in these patterns and our own (deluded and self-congratulatory) power just sinks us in deeper. Still, letting go of attachment to my own imagined progress was very difficult. Had I wasted my time pursuing an impossible goal? Or conversely, was I about to squander all the time and effort I'd put into my quest for enlightenment? Was I succumbing to delusion by abandoning the power of meditation? Finally, I dropped the idea that "I" could attain enlightenment all on my own and released myself to trust in the boundless wisdom and compassion of Amida Buddha. The result was a powerful and lasting peace, joy, and sense of gratitude. My practice and view were transformed and I passed beyond the barrier blocking my path, the obstacle that turned out to be my clinging to an illusionary "self."

Shin taught me to express the deep sense of wonder I'd always felt by saying "thank you" with the practice of chanting *nembutsu,* "Namu Amida Butsu." I began to see that everything I took as my own attainment was actually the working of others: my practice derived from the coming together of the whole universe, of sun and moon and tides, of dirt and plants and honeybees. Rather than an independent being pulling myself up by the bootstraps and seizing my own enlightenment, I realized that I'm the result of the labors of myriad things leading to the present moment in which I'm alive. I breathe in and out, and I'm free to put my arms around my wife and whisper to her.

The essence of Shin is that we're all embraced by Amida's compassionate wisdom, whether or not we experience enlightenment. Therefore we shouldn't worry about *satori* and instead just get on with our lives. The gratitude we express through nembutsu, charity, and other practices are the heart of religious life, not mystical states or hidden knowledge. Laypeople in the Shin tradition don't obsess about constant practice and quick attainment of Buddhahood, the way some lay Zennists tend to. Rather they trust the process, focus on community, gratitude, and charity, and don't try to act enlightened.

The bell rings one last time, and everyone shuffles out quietly. I've spent an hour lost in contemplation, rather than following my breath. Once upon a time I would've berated myself for wasting time, but now I just smile and whisper "Namu Amida Butsu." Shin has given me a new perspective on Zen, allowing me to participate at the zendo without striving for major *kensho* or scolding myself for drifting thoughts. And since my work as a scholar of American Buddhism brings me to many different temples, I'm glad to be able to hang out with folks on both sides of the divide.

Pushing Forward and Standing Still

PHILLIP CRYAN

Late one night while living at a Theravada monastery in northern California, I was reading about Buddhist nonviolent resistance to the Vietnam War. I read of the fierce defiance of Vietnamese nuns, monks, and lay Buddhists standing up to the mass slaughter around them, despite constant persecution and overwhelming odds. My own path in the Dharma had, up until that evening, been largely removed from the world—an inward journey. Inspired by this reading, I resolved to bring Dharma practice into social and political work of my own.

Yet, I had little idea about how to actually do this. In college, I had some taste of political activism when I joined students in attempting to preserve the Ethnic Studies department from budget cuts. But at the time, I was unable to integrate the insights of Dharma with the daily urgencies and complexities of political struggle. I realized I would need to make the transition from solitary practice into political activism gradually, allowing time for new sensibilities to develop, rather than attempting a "grafting" of Dharma principles onto activism. I decided to make this transition

Phillip Cryan, 23, *is a freelance writer and practices primarily in the Chan tradition and Thai forest tradition.*

by focusing on one-on-one relationships through hospice volunteering, with the hopes that I could later build from that into the larger arena of political activism. After a year of learning to "hold the space" of grief in the hospice, and with my university studies coming to an end, I felt I was ready to open to grief on the scale of systemic violence and loss.

I had seen other social activists, without a grounding in wisdom and patience, burn out and falter in the task of uprooting the social structures that multiply suffering. I reflected on the *bodhisattva* of compassion, Kuan Yin. Her resolute, gentle, endless act of liberating—"emptying the ocean with a strand of hair"—captured the feeling of almost unbearably slow progress that arose in doing political work. I wanted to find ways to bring Kuan Yin's example into political expression.

This resolve landed me in Bogotá, Colombia. I worked for Witness for Peace, an organization that brings delegations of U.S. citizens to Latin American countries such as Colombia, Cuba, Nicaragua, and Mexico, to learn firsthand about how U.S. government policies and corporate practices impact those countries. Delegations from Witness for Peace meet with individuals, to hear personal stories about the effects of policy. We then can turn this knowledge, coupled with political and analytical perspectives and tools for activism, into effective movement-building, popular education, and policy-change work at home.

Colombia has been at war for nearly forty years. There are systematic, cold, and grotesque killings. Massacres with chainsaws. Paramilitaries playing soccer with executed men's heads. The U.S. government sends helicopters, weapons, and military trainers to assist the Colombian military in its counterinsurgency, a military with ties to the right-wing paramilitary groups responsible for over seventy percent of civilian deaths each year. I wanted to help build resistance to that U.S. policy.

Colombians who work for justice and peace are threatened, killed, and "disappeared" regularly. The sudden loss of loved ones through murder, kidnapping, or forced exile is an experience shared by most Colombians. The accumulated trauma and grief are vast. It would, I believe, take generations to work through them—assuming, straining the bounds of optimism, that the conflict were to somehow end and new trauma, fear, and loss no longer compounded what people already carry.

Even listening to one person, bearing witness to all of his or her grief and trauma, put to the test all the abilities I thought I'd developed as a Dharma practitioner and activist. One day, at the end of a long series of meetings in a southern Colombian city where guerrillas and paramilitaries carry out regular killings vying for territorial control, we sat down in the office of Pedro, a government human rights official. I was already tired and feeling emotionally bludgeoned by all the horrific stories we'd heard that day.

Pedro spoke without pause for nearly two hours—a hammering, breathless rant, leaving no space for questions or comments from us. He jumped from topic to topic, describing all the awful things going on in the city and in his life, apparently trying to convey the message that there is *nothing* to place hope in.

Pedro had been taken by the paramilitaries a few months before, in reprisal for his denunciations of their human rights violations, and he had been sure that they were going to kill him. When he took the government human rights post a couple years before I met him, Pedro and his wife decided that she and their daughters would be better off far away, so they moved to another province. Yet his wife, a lawyer like Pedro, started receiving death-threats in her new home. She and the girls stopped answering the telephone. The paramilitaries showed Pedro photographs of his daughters entering and leaving their elementary school, photographs of his aging father: shut up, or we will kill everyone you love. "The situation here—and you'll have to forgive my language—is *shit*," Pedro said.

It felt like Pedro's belief in the possibility of justice had just been shattered and that he projected onto us—three twenty-something *gringos*—the now grotesque naiveté of his own former self. His words piled horror upon horror, seemingly trying to produce a sudden recognition that we were laughably deluded, that all institutions have already failed, that security is a myth.

Overwhelmed, I tried to take in Pedro's words. Could I find a way to take his angry slap-across-the-face statements to reveal emptiness in presumed substance, produce the "Aha!" of a Dharma teaching? No, I could not. I was too emotionally confused to tap into that kind of destabilizing wisdom. And there was bitterness in the slap's delivery. So I tried *tonglen,* the Tibetan Buddhist practice of breathing in the smoke of pain and unclarity, breathing out loving-kindness. There were moments of flowing connection, but I couldn't sustain them. I was too tired, scared, and sad. All I could do was to withdraw, to shut myself down emotionally.

The meeting with Pedro took place early in my time working in Colombia. It, together with a series of other events, helped me to begin to see that my idea of unequivocal openness and tonglen-type presence to suffering was misplaced and romantic. A Dharma teacher had warned me years before about the "reckless" use of tonglen. Rather than meeting on the ground of no-self *in difference,* a misguided tonglen simply blurred one's sense of self and of others, attempting to merge. Over my first few months in Colombia, I began to learn that emotional walls could be useful. My responsibility is not to take in others' pain but to focus on the ways in which I can be truly useful in supporting them. And in order to do that effectively, I need to protect my own sanity, strength, and joy.

"Regarding the cries of the world"—Kuan Yin's practice—is not, I've come to believe, about somehow *absorbing* suffering or about blurring distinctions between social and karmic situations, but about the wisdom and precision with which, across varied circumstances, she uses the tools in her ten thousand hands.

I've since learned that whenever I convince myself that I've lost connection to practice altogether, that I've opted for some kind of total immersion program in stress, that the best path out is to focus on the third noble truth rather than the first. It is valuable for me to reflect that there *is* a path out of suffering, not just that *dukkha*, suffering, pervades life. There's much beauty in the difficult activist work we do and in the people with whom we do it— their extraordinary courage, wisdom, and capacity for exuberance despite being faced with daily horrors. If I can for a moment drop the anxiety of feeling there is not enough time to get it all done (and the sense of self that solidifies around it) I can indeed focus on that beauty. This is easier said than done, of course, but it is essentially a simple shift ("a turn of the head is the other shore," as Master Hua, my teacher's teacher, put it).

In a situation where there's not much that we can do to radically change things—in the short-term at least—it is vital that we focus on the good fruits of our efforts, the joys and freeings, the consciousness-shifts and the simple strength in bearing witness. Rather than drawing from a naive hope to fix everything, I find that my political efforts are increasingly grounded in simple dignity, peaceful resistance, and community solidarity. And in all of these values, I find the peace and freedom I need to work diligently and strive for change, while letting go of the need for immediate results and dropping the stress and compulsion. The Buddha calls this "not pushing forward, not standing still."

Last summer I helped lead a delegation of U.S. activists to Colombia. We visited a rural community in a region traditionally held by guerrillas and recently taken by the right-wing paramilitary. It's an area with a long history of organizing, a strong social fabric—one of those beautiful, powerful places in the world where people refuse to be silenced and are willing to pay the consequences of that refusal.

The delegation had been in Colombia for about six days by the time we arrived in the community, and as much as I loved and admired the delegates I was getting tired. Too many nights with too little sleep, the stress of feeling responsible for their safety, the need for vigilance of our surroundings and interactions.

At the end of a day-long community gathering, where the delegates described their past and planned actions in solidarity with Colombians and the community members described the problems they currently face and their tools for resistance, a small group of older men from the community asked to have a closed-door meeting with the delegates. We gathered on wood benches, painted light blue, at the front of the church, and they began to tell their stories.

The sons of these men were killed by paramilitaries a couple years ago, all in one afternoon. For the first time since moving to Colombia, I saw old men weep. As one of them, a community leader for decades, described it, "tears not of fear, but of rage at the injustice". The church-hall had a gentle hush of support and awestruck questioning in it. Compassion filled the space.

The day's heat was beginning to fade, and with it my fatigue lifted. I looked around and saw the tug of powerful emotions on every face: sorrow, rage, compassion, relief, solidarity. Two communities of dignified and open-hearted people, meeting, breaking down—supporting and inspiring one another, strengthening themselves for the years of struggle to come. Joy rose in me, broke through the blunted feelings of tiredness and stress—joy to have been able to serve as a bridge, to see the men's relief in being truly heard, to see the delegates' compassion and strengthened resolve.

At the end of the testimonies we learned that, just after they were shot, the teenage boys' bodies were taken into the church and laid on the same blue benches where we were sitting. We closed with a song, everyone standing, holding hands, weeping freely in sorrow and gratitude.

We pushed forward and we stood still.

RELATIONSHIPS

Mean Street Monk

AJAHN KEERATI CHATKAEW

an oral narrative transcribed by Easton Waller

When I first came to the United States, I didn't really know what I was getting into. I was twenty-four years old and had just graduated from the Buddhist University in Bangkok. That's Thailand's foremost training school for monks. My teacher, Ajahn Phimol Sarapan, wanted to help bring the Dhamma to America and decided to bring me along with him. He said I would play an important role in bringing the Buddha's teachings to the U.S. At the time, I'm not so sure I believed it.

In Thailand, people had told me that Buddhist kids in America have little respect for tradition, that they don't honor their parents, that they join gangs, take drugs, carry guns, shoot each other, and so on. This, also, I didn't really believe.

In fact, during my first few years in America, I saw almost nothing of the horrible things I had been warned about. I stayed at a temple in Richmond, California, for a little more than a year and then at one in Berkeley for about five months. Most of the

Ajahn Keerati Chatkaew, 33, born in northern Thailand, is a Theravada monk working with youth in high-crime areas. Easton Waller, 36, is a Theravada Buddhist, writer, and a professor of comparative religion at Saint Leo University.

kids who came to those places were there with their parents, so, at first, things looked pretty much like they look in Thailand.

Then I moved to downtown Stockton, and suddenly all the stories I had heard were affirmed. Downtown Stockton is a kind of run-down area with a lot of immigrants from Southeast Asia—Thailand, Laos, and Cambodia. There are more Asian gangs here than anywhere else in the United States.

In Thailand, no one would ever think of stealing from a temple, but in Stockton, this was not the case. We had to keep our gate and doors locked at night, because there were times when things were stolen even from the monks. There was gang graffiti everywhere, as well as people passed out on the sidewalks, drive-by shootings, and dealers selling crack right outside the temple gate. I couldn't believe it!

But even though that's the way it was, I felt like I somehow belonged. Ajahn Phimol was right; there was important work to do here, and I could really make a difference.

In Thailand, kids grow up in the Buddhist way. Their schools are Buddhist, their parents are Buddhist, and the king is Buddhist. No matter where you are, you're within walking distance of a temple that houses dozens—even hundreds—of monks. It's the center of the community, and you can go there anytime to pray, to talk with the monks, even just to meet up with people you know.

But obviously it's not like that for the Asian kids of Stockton. They go to school, and everybody speaks English. They learn English better than the language of their parents. Then they come home and they can't always communicate well with their parents. Or they can't relate. Plus, the parents have to work long hours to make ends meet and are gone from the house much of the time. So the kids go out on the streets. But instead of temples and monks, they find guns and drugs. They have few opportunities to learn traditional ways.

So the monks at the Buddhist Temple of Stockton decided to make a place where the kids could be safe from the dangers of the streets and also learn about Buddhism and Asian culture. It wasn't an easy job. The kids knew almost nothing about the way things are done in their traditional lands. They really had no idea how or even why to show respect for monks or their parents or even each other. But we were determined to bring them the Dhamma, so we struggled to find the ways that would work.

There were many unique challenges. For example, we discovered that if there were candies and fruits in front of the Buddha statues that had been placed there as an offering, the little kids wouldn't realize it was an offering. A Thai child would never dream of taking for themselves something that had been offered to the Buddha. But in Stockton, the kids would just go up and take whatever they wanted. How were we to deal with this? First off, we realized we shouldn't be too harsh. In Thailand, monks and parents can be very strict because that's how it is done there. We could have been strict, too. We could have scolded them and told them they're not allowed to have the treats because they were being disrespectful. But, instead, we said, "Sure, you can have whatever you want. But you've got to ask a monk first if it's okay. And then you've got to bow three times in front of the Buddha. After that, it's yours." In this way we taught tradition and respect.

Also, we let the kids hang out whenever they wanted. They could come to the temple at any time. They could play basketball, listen to hip-hop music, "kick it with their homies," whatever they wanted, as long as they had the monks' approval. We discovered it was important to make them feel at home, because if we were too strict, they wouldn't come here *at all*. And then they would never receive *any* Dhamma teachings. This way, they come to us of their own free will. We had to show them that there were benefits to coming to the temple.

We also had to show them that everything is a matter of cooperation—even the way we talk. If I expect them to learn Pali chants and Asian languages, then I should be willing to learn the way they talk, too. So I call them "dawg" and "homie." I even tease them sometimes and call them "the crackheads"—never in a mean way, only to make them laugh. They think it's funny to hear a monk who knows all those words, and we even came up with a joke that the temple is like a gang. The monks are the O.G.s (for those of you who may not know, that stands for Original Gangstas). The gang color is yellow, like the monks' robes. To get "jumped in," you've got to learn a chant. We call it "the Yellow Gang."

Eventually, more and more kids started coming to the temple. There were lots of Laotian and Cambodian kids in the neighborhood, so the parking lot became a playground. Everybody knew that the temple had an open-door policy and that it was a safe place where there were never any guns or drugs. The monks became like substitute parents for the kids. We helped them with their homework, taught them how to speak Thai and Laotian and Cambodian. We set things up like a big family. In fact, several of the older boys practically lived at the temple. They came from families with lots of kids and their houses were very crowded. So, they'd sleep at the temple. And that meant they had a responsibility to clean up after themselves. All the kids would work together to cook and clean and run errands. And the big kids had a special responsibility to look after the little kids. The monks were like the parents of the house. They also worked but had the special job of laying down the rules and making sure everything ran smoothly.

In fact, we became so much like parents that we sometimes had to be very tough for the kids' own good. In one case, one of the older boys had become very rude with the monks and with the other kids. After ten years of practically living at the temple, he suddenly refused to do any chore work and would ignore people whenever they tried to talk to him. This went on for weeks.

I asked him what was wrong, but all he would say is, "I don't know."

Finally, after he said this several times, I said, "Well, if *you* don't know, who *does?*"

Guess how he answered? You guessed it: "I don't know."

That's when I decided to be very direct with him. I told him that he is in control of his own life. Nobody else. Therefore, he really ought to know what's bothering him—especially if it's bothering him so much that he could totally disrespect the people who have been there for him his whole life.

At first, he was angry. He said he didn't really fit in at the temple any more and that he didn't see why he should stick around. He said there was no reason for him to show respect to anyone at the temple because no one there ever showed any respect to him.

"Okay," I said. "If that's the way you feel, that's fine with me. The only thing I ask of you is not to come here any more if that's the way you really feel. It doesn't make sense for you to come here if you dislike it so much."

He looked like he was going to cry, and I could tell he was finally ready to start being honest. As it turns out, he had been dating a girl whom he really liked a lot, and one of his best friends had started dating her behind his back. To make matters worse, all the other teenagers knew what the unfaithful friend was doing.

"Okay," I said, "now I understand. And I would also understand if you don't ever want to come here again. That would be okay. But think about this: if you never come back here again, then all the time the monks have spent teaching you has gone to waste. Why? Because what we were teaching you is the traditional Buddhist way. And the traditional Buddhist way is respect for the people in your life. How long have you been coming here? Ten years? That's a lot of history. And where we come from it's important to honor your history. If a person or a group of people stick with you for ten years, that's dedication. And you owe it to them to show them the same amount of dedication—out of gratitude, out of respect. Think about it. Do you really want to throw away ten years of friendship and instruction in a single minute?"

Then I called the friend over. I asked if it was really true that he had been dating the girl that his best friend loved. He said it was. I asked if he thought that was fair to his buddy. He said his friend shouldn't be so upset because it was no big thing. He said he wasn't serious with the girl and was just having fun. I was just as direct with him as I had been with his buddy. I told him, "Don't ever toy with a woman like that. Women deserve to be respected, not treated as fun toys. If you're serious, that's one thing. But if you're just fooling around, that's another. Never treat a girl like that. And never treat your friend like that either."

At any rate, I think our dedication to the kids of this community has paid off. The two boys are best friends again, and many of the kids who used to be in gangs have gotten out and now spend their spare time at the temple. Some have thanked us and told us that we changed their lives. They've even shown us that they're as dedicated to us as we are to them. For example, we lost our old building last year in a long legal battle that was very damaging to the community. Now, even though we live in a small rental house that's several miles away from the old neighborhood, many of the kids from "the 'hood" still come and visit us. Even though it's not easy for them to get out here, they still find a way to honor their teachers. They want to keep the Yellow Gang alive. It represents the opposite of everything the other gangs stand for. Instead of addiction, it's freedom. Instead of violence, it's peace. Instead of death, it's life. That's the Buddha's way. And the fact that they want to keep it going makes us very proud of them. Because there's history there. And history deserves respect.

Black Is Buddhafull

BHIKSUNI THICH CHAN CHAU NGHIEM

My brother and I didn't meet our grandparents, our dad's parents, until I was eight. It was the summer of 1982 and our parents had just divorced. Our mom is black, our dad is white.

My dad had seriously disappointed his white, upper-class, Texan parents when he joined the Civil Rights movement. They were completely alienated and enraged when he decided to marry a black woman in Chicago in 1970. I think he saw them only once or twice after this until he and my mom divorced. My mom's family was much more accepting. My black grandma came to help my mom with me right after I was born, and I grew up visiting my mom's side of the family regularly.

We drove from Chicago to Houston to meet my other grandparents. They were kind to us, happy to meet their only grandchildren. They let us go out shopping with their housekeeper and she got us whatever we wanted. My granddad gave my dad money to take us to Six Flags and Waterworld. We sat in the den with him and listened to him tell stories as he smoked cigars. His easy chair was full of holes from cigar ash that fell when he got too sleepy. He

Bhiksuni Thich Chan Chau Nghiem (Kaira Lingo), 28, is a nun in the Vietnamese Zen tradition of Thich Nhat Hanh.

had a deep throaty chuckle and loved to tell jokes. I also enjoyed asking my grandma questions and listening to her share about her life. I wanted to love them, and it wasn't difficult. I saw their care for my dad and his love for them. I was shocked and hurt though, when my granddad told a story about a "nigger." He didn't seem to be at all aware of what he'd said, or at least how it sounded to us. My jaw dropped and I turned to my brother for help, whispering "did you hear what he just said?" All three of us bristled, and I think granddad kept to "nigra" or "colored" after that.

About three years ago, my dad and I attended a twenty-one-day retreat with Thich Nhat Hanh and the Plum Village Sangha in Vermont. My granddad had died ten years earlier. One day I was doing sitting meditation in the gymnasium turned meditation hall. Thich Nhat Hanh, also called *Thay* (the Vietnamese word for "teacher"), had been giving teachings on Touching the Earth, a practice in which we connect with our ancestors to heal the suffering in our relationships and to strengthen the goodness they have passed on to us. Often as an adult, I had reflected with bitterness on my grandparents' racism and their refusal to accept their only grandchildren for at least eleven or twelve years (my older brother's age when we first met them). They rejected their own son and missed out on most of our childhood. I hated that my dad wouldn't have brought us to meet them if he were still married to my mom. In their eyes, the divorce was an admission of defeat, an acknowledgment that they had been right all along. Only under these conditions could we come into their lives.

I sat and breathed to connect with my granddad. "Breathing in, granddad, I am here for you. Breathing out, I will take good care of you in me." Soon I was in tears. Up came a very deep, old hurt of feeling rejected, discriminated against, unloved because of my skin color. It was very painful. But I had never embraced this pain with my mindfulness before. It had just been lying there, stuck in my consciousness. Now it could circulate freely, massaged by mindful breathing. I held my pain—this feeling that I had missed out on something important as a little girl—with tenderness and love and allowed the hot tears to flow down my cheeks.

As I held and began to release this block of pain and confusion, I meditated on my granddad, and began to look deeply into him. I felt his presence very strongly. Suddenly I knew he didn't *want* to be the way he was, in fact he made himself suffer tremendously because of his rigid beliefs about race. And I saw that it would have been very difficult for him to have thought or acted differently given the way he was raised and the consciousness of his generation. He could never fathom an interracial marriage and certainly not of his own son. I felt a deep sense of connectedness with him as I continued to breathe and I felt in the marrow of my bones that he loved my brother and me deeply, from the moment we were born, but was unable to express it until years later. And that he deeply regretted this. I knew that it caused him real pain to be caught in this way of thinking and not be able to get out.

I see now that our presence in his life was also an opening, an opportunity for him to be more inclusive and to let go of some of his long-held beliefs. If he hadn't been able to do this at least to some extent, he wouldn't have even let us in the door. He loved to watch my brother play around. My granddad had been a football player and a coach and he appreciated my brother's athletic strength and agility. I think he saw something of himself in this brown grandson of his.

As I sat, I felt a deep communication between us. He let me know how proud he was of what I was doing, of all that I had done. He was happy that I had found a path of beauty and understanding that could transform the many generations of suffering in our family. I felt him very much alive in me. I knew I was his continuation and I vowed to live my life deeply to honor him and all the good qualities he had passed down to me—his persever-ance, his calm, his thoughtfulness, his way of connecting to peo-ple, his general goodness. I kept crying and crying—it was so beautiful to feel this love, this comforting and full warmth spread-ing through my chest, finally releasing this heavy burden of igno-rance, separation, and pain. In its place I felt a lightness, a deeper confidence in myself, in the practice of mindfulness and in a very real connectedness with my ancestors. I let go of the judgment and resentment that I had always carried in my heart toward him. I loved him unreservedly, and for the first time I felt truly happy to be his granddaughter.

After that retreat, I went on to ordain as a novice nun in the tradition of Thich Nhat Hanh. A few months into my novitiate, I wrote Thay a letter about wanting to integrate my blackness more into my practice, to embrace it and make room for it. Most of the time in our community I just feel like a Westerner, because most of the brothers and sisters in the community are Vietnamese. But when black people come to visit us, I see myself and identify more strongly as black, not just Western. I want to connect with them as a fellow black practitioner. I had a feeling of love and attraction to black people, but also felt conflict about how to express that feel-ing, how to relate to it. I felt unsure of myself and wondered if it was appropriate to reach out to someone just on the basis of race. And at the same time, it felt so important to meet each other on that level as well as all the other levels of our personality. I wrote to Thay that I felt I needed to affirm, understand, and nurture this part of me more.

Some weeks later, Thay visited us in the Lower Hamlet of Plum Village. He called all the ordained women together and served us tea and sweets. He had asked us some time ago to paint the outside of the sisters' building, because it looked pretty old and gray. As we hadn't done anything about it yet, he decided to motivate us some by asking us to go around in a circle and each say which color we'd like the building to be. The sisters answered quickly with blue or pink or a natural tone. When it got to my turn, I hesitated.

Suddenly, Thay broke the silence, "Black is Beautiful!"

I couldn't believe he said that! The other sisters burst out laughing.

It was only later that I connected his response to the letter I had written him. It was unexpected in a very affirming and deep way. He didn't respond directly to what I wrote, but this answer gave me real nourishment and a great deal to think about. I felt really seen. I felt he was trying to tell me that I didn't need to work so hard to understand or figure things out. I just needed to practice, to enjoy myself and then I would naturally touch the beauty in my heritage—not through struggling, but by allowing my mind to settle down and be in the present moment. I felt he understood me so perfectly and helped me to get out of old, stuck ways of thinking with real lightness and grace. His declaration is a kind of *koan* for me, a teaching that I can always come back to, to find deeper and deeper layers of meaning. Who am I? What is it about me that is black? How, why is it beautiful? How can I help that beauty manifest?

I have kept these questions in mind. On a recent visit to my brother and his family in Washington D.C., some thoughts became clearer. My sister-in-law and I were driving my nephew to school—his first month in pre-kindergarten. He pointed out the homeless people on the street and asked me if I give them money when I see them. I told him, "Sometimes." A few days later when I was returning from an errand, a homeless man asked me to buy him some dinner. He was standing in front of a restaurant. I surprised myself saying, "Sure!" and went in to get him a plate of fried catfish and vegetables. I told my four-year-old nephew about it that night as I was reading him a bedtime story. He asked me immediately, "Auntie, was he black or white?"

Why do four-year-old black children have to ask that? How is it that they already know that it matters, that it has consequences for them? I answered, unwillingly, "Black." He was quiet. I don't think white children feel compelled to know things like this. Being black is already painful, right from the beginning.

Contemplating what it is about me that is black, I remember that I used to squeeze the bridge of my nose for hours as a young girl, hoping my nose would become skinny like a white person's. In 2002, when I learned the D.C. snipers were black, I was ashamed and scared. Their acts were one more reason for society to hate and fear black people. I was afraid in an almost unconscious way of some collective racial punishment. When they caught the snipers, somehow it was *me* that was caught, every black person was implicated. My blackness is fear, insecurity on a cellular level, transmitted by my ancestors.

What is black about me is also an indescribable feeling of *home*, sitting around the dining room table at my grandma's eating Sunday dinner and listening to my family talk, argue, laugh, and just be themselves. My blackness is also the way I can feel one with my body, the way *I am* the music when I dance. My mother, grandmother, great-grandmother, all the women on my mom's side, were natural dancers. They just had to see a move once and they could do it, effortlessly. That is deep wisdom. My blackness is the way I get chills when I listen to certain spirituals or gospel singing in a black church. My blackness is a deep desire for wholeness and for non-fear.

For the beauty of my blood ancestors to manifest as fully as possible in my life, I have to heal their suffering that continues on in me—the fear, the self-negation. Touching the strength of my spiritual ancestors in Buddhism is helping me to do this.

Generations of Buddhist practitioners were able to transform profound ignorance and suffering in themselves and bring their insight into the world to transform others, and to transform social injustice. This is tremendous food for my *bodhicitta,* my deep desire to love. I feel gratitude for the Buddha's openness in welcoming "Untouchables" into the *sangha,* as well as his decision to allow women to ordain. I am inspired by the Buddha's wisdom to ordain the serial killer Angulimala who then became an exemplary monk. These were revolutionary actions, breaking through the deeply rooted social limitations of his time. This tradition continues. I see the same ability to transform social barriers and heal injustice in my teacher and my sangha.

Thich Nhat Hanh teaches that when we ordain as a monastic, nothing is lost, everything we have done or experienced in the past is still a part of us and can be helpful to us on our path. I know that part of who I am is a person of color who very much wants to be an instrument of the Dharma in healing racism. While living in such an international community as Plum Village in France, I didn't think much about race. Since I have returned to the U.S., I find myself back in familiar and painful racial territory. I have been saddened by how few people of color attended our retreats. I have a deep aspiration to help our retreats become more economically accessible and racially diverse, with more black, Latino, and Native American participants. I want to bring more of the beauties of black culture into our monastic life through singing, dance, poetry, sharing our history, and connecting with young people. I want to sing in a Buddhist gospel choir!

I am coming to understand my need to connect to people of color, just to enjoy being ourselves together and to help each other integrate our Buddhist practice with our experience as people of color. At my first U.S. retreat with Thay and the sangha as a monastic, we held a dinner gathering for retreatants of color and their friends and family. This was another kind of homecoming for me. I was so happy to meet and practice mindfulness with other people of color. I was touched when they expressed their joy in being with a monastic of black heritage. They felt more connected to our monastic sangha and our tradition because there was someone like them in it.

Recently I have read several books and articles by black Dharma teachers, like Jan Willis, Ralph Steele, Alice Walker, and Angel Kyodo Williams. It is encouraging to know there are actually a lot of them out there! They are bringing the black experience into the Dharma and the Dharma is better for it. Currently, in our global Plum Village Sangha we are beginning to raise awareness about the absence of people of color in our retreats and local sanghas. Thay has agreed to offer a retreat for people of color, our first ever. We have plans to set up a fund to help more people of color attend our retreats and to encourage our largely white local sanghas to engage in diversity and healing racism efforts. It is heartening to see this awakening happening in other Dharma centers and sanghas. We are just at the beginning. When I think of the power of engaged Dharma, I know that my nephew's generation has a chance at living in a very different America. It is up to us.

Born to a Born-Again Mother

KIM COLLINS MORENO

My husband and I had a traditional American Zen Buddhist wedding. Well…as traditional Zen Buddhist as it could be, given that it was held in the Cathedral of the Incarnation, one of Baltimore's older and more imposing Episcopal churches. Actually, we were the second Buddhist couple to have a wedding in the parish hall: there had been another one about a year before. So there was a precedent.

The day before the wedding, Kevin and I spent the day in the parish hall setting up rows of cushions for meditations and an altar. Both our mothers helped with setting up the flowers and the candles. My nine-year-old niece, our ring-bearer, dutifully lint-brushed all the *zabutons*, like any good Zen student does at the end of a sitting. Our priest, Jishu Sensei, a married American woman ordained in the Soto lineage, drove down from Yonkers to officiate.

On the wedding day, each party approached the altar, bowed and then took their seats. When we had rehearsed this the day before, my mother had announced, "I'm not bowing to that

Kim Collins Moreno, 32, has been practicing Zen for ten years and is an archivist for the State of Maryland.

altar!" I said, "Okay." Right before the wedding ceremony, my mother repeated this to me and to Jishu. Jishu said, "Okay."

My mother is a fundamentalist Christian. She believes that you must accept the Lord Jesus Christ as your personal Lord and Savior in order to be saved and escape eternal damnation and torment. She believes that Jesus Christ will return like a thief in the night and those who are saved shall be transported to heaven in the blink of an eye. She believes that we will experience the Last Days on Earth, an Antichrist will walk among us, and we will endure days of Tribulation before the Final Battle in which the Devil is defeated forever and tossed into the Lake of Fire.

In fact, it had taken a lot of courage for her to just be there at our wedding, just as it had taken a lot of courage for me to have the wedding that was true for me and Kevin. My mother had given me a small white Bible passed down through the generations that she had saved for my wedding day. She wanted me to carry it beneath my bouquet. I knew how much it meant to her, and I didn't want to hurt her by refusing. But I also felt it would be dishonest for me to carry that Bible. So I said to her, "It would mean a lot to me if *you* carried the Bible in the procession." I thought that would have been a better expression of both our faiths.

Once we were all seated and the incense lit, Jishu began speaking. She had taken care to make our vows inclusive and feminist. After Jishu spoke, Kevin and I made full prostrations to the altar, in gratitude to the Three Treasures, to our ancestors and parents, to our friends, and to all beings in the animal, vegetable, and mineral worlds. We chanted the *gatha* of atonement, a chant in which we ritually acknowledge all of our past harmful *karma*. Jishu took a pine branch, dipped it in water, brushed it over her head, then over Kevin's head and my head. Then Kevin and I stood and took vows to practice the Buddhist precepts: not to kill, not to steal, to refrain from sexual misconduct, not to lie, and to abstain from abusing intoxicants. My niece came shyly forward and offered us our wedding rings, plain silver bands on a white cushion.

Then Kevin and I stood facing our guests and offered poems we had chosen for the occasion. I recited Pablo Neruda's Sonnet XVII. Kevin read my favorite poem, Gary Snyder's "The Blue Sky." Kevin's mother read Richard Wilbur's "A Wedding Toast."

Next was my mother's turn to read the selection she had chosen for the occasion. Her voice shook as she loudly proclaimed, "I am going to read from the Holy Word of God." My heart started beating faster, and my breath came up short. I had become accustomed to inwardly preparing myself to withstand the power of my mother witnessing. That's what she was doing—reaching out to this gathering, which must have looked very foreign and heathen to her. She was piercing the darkness with the Holy Word of God.

Earlier in the day, Kevin had quietly chastised me after he had overheard my response to my mother when she had asked for an explanation of one of the ceremonial items Jishu held. My mother had pointed to the white horsehair fly whisk, a symbol of spiritual authority, which represents the hair of the Buddha. "What is that strange thing she's holding? That's weeeeiiiirrrdd," my mother said, drawing out the word. Without hesitation, and with a bit of a shrug, I answered, "Oh. That's her fly whisk. It's the hair of the Buddha. It's to chase away the demons. We don't want any demons at our wedding ceremony, do we?" Kevin took me aside as we filled our incense bowls in the parish kitchen. "Kim, you should take it easy on your mother! She already thinks this whole ceremony is heathen. You didn't need to talk about demons!"

Now, my mother prepared to read from the Holy Word of God. Her hands gripped tightly the small white Bible. She read from Ephesians:

And be ye kind one to another, tender-hearted, forgiving one another, even as God for Christ's sake hath forgiven you…. Wives, submit yourselves unto your own husbands, as unto the Lord. For the husband is the head of the wife, even as Christ is the head of the church: and he is the savior of the body. Therefore as the church is subject unto Christ, so let the wives be to their own husbands in every thing. Husbands, love your wives, even as Christ also loved the church, and gave himself for it.

I glanced around the room, at the faces of the guests gathered there. I saw looks of discomfort, shock, disapproval, and embarrassment. But *I* didn't feel any of those emotions. At that moment, I felt love, compassion, and pride for my mother. I was profoundly grateful that my mother loved me so much that she would be there for me on that day, in that place, amid all the Buddhist robes and chanting and incense.

Later, as Kevin and I stood greeting our guests in the receiving line, my godmother said, "That was the most beautiful wedding ceremony I've ever seen. That was really uncomfortable, though, when your mother read that 'wives submit yourselves to your husbands' thing." I said, "Yeah." What else could I say? I was simply glad my mother was at my wedding. That she showed up at all was a testament to her faith, to who she is, and to the complicated blend of emotions that tie us together.

My Sunday School teachers, youth ministers, and parents did a pretty good job of raising a good Christian girl. I went to Bible study on Wednesday nights, Sunday School and church on Sunday mornings, followed by anointed prayer meetings and fellowship on Sunday evenings. I attended youth group meetings, Christian summer camps, and Petra concerts. I could recite the books of the Bible, in order, and can quote scripture on command. But I wasn't content with mere "churchianity," as my pastor said in his sermons. I needed a faith that was fully lived, daily, through my whole being. Evangelism was just the wrong faith.

Back before I had discovered Zen, I had felt I owed it to my Christian heritage to give it one more shot. I had checked out a pile of books on Quaker history and thought that, if any Christian denomination would be right for me, it would be the Society of Friends of Jesus. I spent a little over a year attending Quaker meetings each Sunday. I still love the Quakers, but the fact remains that I am not a Christian, Quaker or otherwise. Then after reading instructions in Philip Kapleau's *The Three Pillars of Zen,* I began sitting *zazen* alone in my room. I promised myself that if I sat every morning and evening for thirty minutes for one month straight, I would buy a *zafu* and *zabuton.*

My zafu and zabuton, ordered from Shasta Abbey, arrived in the mail on a Saturday morning. My mother brought the big box from the porch to my bedroom and said, "You got this big box in the mail." She was obviously anxious to see what it was. I said, "Oh! My cushions!" I tore into the box. My mother breathed a huge sigh of relief. "Oh thank GOD," she said. "You just ordered some pretty cushions for your bedroom. I thought you had ordered a big Buddha statue and you were going to bow down and worship it!"

My mother would sometimes walk into my room while I was sitting zazen. "Oh, I'm sorry, Hon. I didn't realize you were exercising." For my mother, prayer has specific forms: petitionary prayer, preferably on your knees, at your bedside each night and every morning; prayer at the altar when you are deeply contrite and in need of salvation; anointed prayer to pray for special healing for someone who is ill. This last type of prayer I find actually very moving and beautiful. I am reminded of it when we recite a particular piece of Zen liturgy, the Sho Sai Myo Kichijo Dharani, and the chant leader intones:

We pray for the health and well-being of: All those afflicted by diseases of body, mind, or spirit; all those working towards the healing of those afflictions. We especially pray for....

Both are powerful community prayers for healing.

When I was a little girl, I had pneumonia. One Sunday night, my mother came to my sickbed, where I was covered with a quilt my grandmother had made especially for me. My mother sat on my bed, held my hands in hers, and told me that she and my father had participated in anointed prayer for my healing.

A few weeks ago, I recited the Kanzeon *sutra* and prayers to the Medicine Buddha for my mother. She was going in for an operation. I took a week off from work so I could take her to her pre-op testing, take her to the hospital for her surgery, and stay with her during her recuperation. The night before her surgery, I slept in my old bedroom, where I had once set up a Buddha-less altar on a bookcase. Now, I was lying in bed, silently doing loving-kindness meditation. I extended the loving-kindness meditation especially to my mother that she might be calm for her surgery and heal quickly and fully.

The next morning, my aunt arrived at the house at six in the morning to pray with my mother. I did morning yoga in my mother's bedroom, so I would not disturb my aunt and my mother praying in the living room. As I moved through the various poses, the sounds of their prayers floated through the hallway and into the room. I could hear my aunt, with her slight Kentucky accent, praying fervently. I could hear my mother responding, "Yes, Jesus. Yes, Lord."

Later that morning, as my mother and I waited in the pre-op room for the doctor to arrive, my mother asked me if I could teach her some of my "yoga exercises" sometime. I said, "Well, we could do some breathing exercises right now. Would you like to?" I asked her to put her hands lightly on her abdomen and feel the rise and fall of her belly as she breathed. I asked her to breathe deeply, slowly and fully, to feel her belly swell as she inhaled. I noticed how sharp and short her breath was, and wondered if she had ever taken a full, deep breath in her life. I then sat with her as we both breathed together, focusing on our breath. After a few moments of silence, the doctor entered the room.

My mother recovered beautifully.

—————————

In the Hollywood movie of my life, there would be this wonderful reconciliation at the end, where my mother and I would have a long, heartfelt talk about our respective faiths. She would come to understand my faith and why it sustains me. I would be able to tell her how she did such a good job raising a daughter who sought the things of the spirit rather than the things of the flesh. I would reveal to her just how deeply I had come to appreciate and understand Christianity as my Buddhist practice deepened.

But I don't share this with my mother. We don't talk about religion much at all. Jesus said, "Ye shall know them by their fruits. Do men gather grapes of thorns, or figs of thistles? Even so every good tree bringeth forth good fruit.... Wherefore by their fruits ye shall know them." As I learned in my fundamentalist, Christian family, you do not talk about your religion. You live it every day.

Dangerous Thoughts

TENZIN DORJEE

When I was five years old, being a good Buddhist meant getting up at five o'clock every day to attend the morning prayers. My friends and I did more playing than praying, of course. When I was ten, being a good Buddhist meant letting my classmates copy my homework, eating carefully so as not to waste any food, and watching my steps in order to avoid squashing unfortunate insects.

I grew up in a Tibetan school, located in a beautiful valley in northern India, called Patlikuhl. All day long my classmates and I played games behind a dilapidated house that served as the school temple. Our favorite game was shooting Chinese soldiers. Each of us carried a fake wooden gun and pretended to be a Tibetan guerrilla warrior. Although no one played the role of Chinese soldiers, we hunted down imaginary ones and shot them anyway. To a young Tibetan boy, nothing felt dissonant about being Buddhist and killing Chinese soldiers.

When I became a teenager, morning prayers were replaced by morning meditations. Now I was watching not only my steps but

Tenzin Dorjee, 22, *a graduate of Tibetan Children's Village and Brown University, is currently working at the National Endowment for Democracy, Washington, D.C., and is on the board of directors of Students for a Free Tibet.*

also my breath. Killing Chinese soldiers did not seem right any more, even though it was just a game. Being Buddhist was no longer child's play but a man's struggle.

A Buddhist should love all sentient beings, elders told me. A Buddhist should love even his enemies. I had no enemy—except, of course, the one billion Chinese who had invaded my homeland. Well, good disciple that I was, I crossed my legs, closed my eyes, and contemplated compassion for my enemies.

These Chinese invaders are not your enemies. They are a poor people, of a poor land, living in a spiritual void. They are only victims of their own government. Do not hate them, but feel sorry for them. Breathe in their sorrow, breathe out your joy to them. Breathe in. Breathe out. In. Out. Why, they were your own mothers in your previous lives! Be kind to them. Forgive them. Give them your love, give them your happiness….

And give them Tibet, my land, too?

No, not your land. Fight for your land, but fight with love instead of hate. Breathe in. Breathe out. Yes, love, peace, compassion, these will bring lasting freedom and happiness to the Tibetan people.

Whom am I trying to fool? Love, peace, and compassion: aren't these what cost us our freedom? Love, peace, and compassion did not stop the Chinese from invading us.

Stop! This thought is dangerous!

I took a deep breath in and tried to relax.

Compassion never killed anyone. Compassion is the virtue that frees a person from bondage. Oh, these are the teachings of the Buddha, the very practice of which has made your people peaceful and your land unique. How dare you, how dare you condemn this religion which is the soul of the land you love? Remember, oh disciple of the Buddha, that this fight is not about such material things as land and resources.

What? What am I fighting for if not for the land?

You are not fighting for the land, but for the six million Tibetans to whom the land means a great deal. If you fight for the land, you will be swept away by delusions such as attachment and hate. But if you fight for the people, the goodness of the end will guide you on to the right path.

Oh no, where is my meditation? Am I not supposed to calm my mind down and stop all thoughts? Do I realize that without meditation there is no nirvana? Why is it that I cannot meditate properly for even five minutes? At this rate, I will never attain nirvana!

But look, it is already time for breakfast!

I opened my eyes. At the same time, I closed my mind to the dangerous thoughts of going to war to free my homeland. I stood up, stretched my legs, and ran downstairs to breakfast.

———————

I have lived in America for the last five years, a new home. I am now both an old boy and a young man. I still watch my breath often and my footsteps constantly. I consider that beneath my feet crawl creatures that, like me, breathe in and out. They may or may not be meditating, but they are living. These days, I believe in the teachings of the Buddha, but I follow them more selectively than I did when I was a kid. So sometimes I wonder if I am still a Buddhist.

I still meditate. Meditation is stopping all thoughts, elders tell me. Meditation is being in the moment, elders tell me. I still, even as a young adult with some years of practice, find it hard to live up to these ancestral standards. My thoughts naturally leave my meditation and escape to the mountains of Tibet. Oh, how I miss the land that I have never seen!

Breathe in. Breathe out. In. Out. Breathe into yourself the sorrow of all beings in samsara. Breathe out to them your love and happiness. Breathe into yourself the suffering even of those who torture your people in Tibet. Breathe out your compassion and forgiveness toward them.

I stop myself.
Can I breathe out something that does not exist inside me?

Yes, yes, the moment you breathe it out, it will come to be.
Oh! Magic, huh?
This is no laughing matter! They took your land with violence, but you will take it back in peace. The moment you pick up arms, you become the very evil you seek to destroy. After all, you want your homeland back so that you can preserve your religion! Is this not so?
This is so, this is so.
And your religion is nothing but kindness!
I know, I know. But how kind should I be? As kind as the Buddha?
By all means. Being a Buddhist means imitating the Buddha until you become a buddha yourself.
Well, what would the Buddha do if someone took his land by force? Why, he would smile and ask, "What else do you want?" So, tell me, should I be as kind as the Buddha?
Uh, um…it is difficult to say, very difficult.
See? Don't you see? When one man practices what the

Buddha taught, he ends his suffering. But when a whole people practices what the Buddha taught, they end themselves.

Be careful what you say. More importantly, be careful what you think. And yes, watch your breath.

But how? How can I sit here and watch my breath rise and fall when things are falling apart, never to rise again, in my homeland? How can I talk of love and kindness when my people have known nothing but fear and destruction for five decades?

Be calm and think. Revenge will only bring more fear and destruction. You will fight for Tibetan freedom, but not at the cost of Buddhist principles. You will fight for your people, but not at the cost of other people. You must not forget, oh disciple of the Buddha, that the struggle for your homeland is a religious struggle, that peace is the ultimate weapon.

Peace is good, but is it strong? Love makes us divine, but isn't it anger that keeps us alive?

Ah, I am confused. I am so confused!

I slowly open my eyes. This time, my mind, instead of closing, remains open even as I end the meditation. The dangerous thoughts that were lurking in the dark recesses of my mind are out in the open. They cannot run anywhere. I face them squarely. I do not understand them yet, but I take pride in having them out in the open and examining them. My confusion has turned into curiosity.

What's Crazy, Really?

LAYLA MASON

"I've got a cold, so I won't be coming to morning meditation tomorrow," my brother said over the phone. We were both students at the same college. "I'm going to sleep in and shake it off; so just carry on without me." The next morning, trudging through sludgy snow from my dorm toward the chapel meditation room, I passed my brother's freshman dorm, thought about his being sick, and decided to check in on him. Everyone was still sleeping, but his door was half-way open. I came into a room that was impeccably clean. In fact, all that was in it was the pale pine college furniture and a Douglas Adams book in the desk. Even the trash was empty.

My brother came in the door, I guess from the bathroom. His eyes were googling all over the place, and he could barely walk. I thought he might be drunk. "What's the matter?" He grunted something unintelligible and began weaving all over the room. "Come here and breathe out," I demanded, not sure of what vapor he'd emit. No alcohol. What was going on? I began to panic; he was clearly out of his mind. I called Dad and then the

Layla Mason, 26, is writing under a pseudonym.

campus police. An officer and I carried him out to a patrol car and to the college clinic. In the psychiatrist's room, my brother began climbing on the furniture like a drugged ape and drooling on himself. The clinic called an ambulance and we took him to the hospital, strapped down on a stretcher.

The blood tests showed no irregular substances in his blood. After an overnight stay at the hospital, where I slept miserably in the lounge, the psychiatrist said he probably had a dissociative incident brought on by the stress of final exams. He was fine to return to college. When I got back to his dorm room, I found a note in the Adams book, *Life, the Universe, and Everything.* "Please return this book to my friend I borrowed it from. I've decided to end my life, and now I'm gone. I'm sorry if I've caused any pain."

This was my brother's first suicide attempt, through vodka and a new brand of sleeping pill, which inaugurated five years of hospitalizations, group homes, therapy, and medications—and it changed forever what it meant for me to be his closest friend. The most distressing part of my brother's sudden change from high school valedictorian, likeable, athletic young man, was that I didn't know *why* it had happened. The doctors said it was most likely a biological predisposition to schizophrenia that often emerges at around eighteen, especially upon leaving the structured environment of a home. My dad was pretty happy with that answer, as it left everyone blameless but the genes. But there was another possible explanation.

The doctors asked me to give an extensive history of our childhood. I began telling them what had never been discussed before outside the family: that my father had been a violent and unpredictable parent for the last ten years that we'd been living with him. The beatings for small things like forgetting to lock the back door, the spit on our faces, the hundreds of pushups for repentance of being disrespectful, the million little mind games, his paranoia of the outside world. The doctors began to change their diagnosis: we think your brother may have post traumatic stress disorder, they told me. My brother, after a decade of living in terror that this man would make good on his threats to "throw him out the window" and "break every bone in his body," had turned all of my father's rage inside toward himself.

The doctors sitting around the long table in the florescent-lit room were looking at me quietly, no longer writing on their yellow legal pads, as I finished telling them the truth. It felt good to tell the truth. As I did, it dawned on my nineteen-year-old brain that these stories were horrifying. And then I realized what they were thinking: how could I, who not only witnessed but experienced these things, have not gone crazy myself? I had straight A's at college, was seemingly well-adjusted, dating—and visiting my Thorazine-drugged, drooling brother every few weeks in the pink-painted locked ward.

Over the years, while my brother got worse, I did everything I could to prove to myself that I was not like him, that I would never become like him. I graduated with high honors, while he was slicing himself with the top of a soda can in the state hospital. I went to graduate school, while he attempted to set himself on fire at the group home. I got published, while he tried to shoot his eyes out with a BB gun. While my brother was dealing with our past by destroying himself, I dealt with it by becoming an overachiever.

But I was not ashamed that I had a brother like this. In fact, I wore the My Crazy Brother Story on my already-decorated coat like a badge of honor: not only was I a successful person, but I had become so *despite* circumstances that drove another person insane. What's more, I could tell people that I had devoted hundreds of hours to his care, arranging doctors, playing the mental health system, even letting him live with me for a summer. I told our story over and over and felt good when people said, "How did you do it? You are so strong for someone so young."

Then, this last summer, something happened that put a small fissure in this thick wall I'd built between myself and my brother, between sanity and insanity. I encountered a Zen master. Daeheng Sunim is now in her late seventies. She's known as a powerful teacher, psychic, and leader of the enormous, wealthy international Zen organization that she founded. In a rare opportunity, I was able to interview with her when I was visiting Seoul. To prepare well for the meeting, I began reading her biography.*

Sunim's life began as terribly as ours: a violent and hyper-controlling father, a yielding and unprotective mother, living in poor and dirty conditions. Her father's abuse forced her to run away to the woods to sleep at night. Between the lines, I wondered if her father was a predator at night especially. When she reached young adulthood, she finally ran away from home for good, became a nun, and entered the forest for ten years of practice. Wandering around in winter in light cotton robes, eating leaves and grass, Sunim slept under pine trees and meditated in a hole dug in the sand near a river. Her skin was cracked and bleeding, her bones sticking out, her wild hair tied up in a ball with a stick. Her *koan* became *Appa!* or "Daddy!" in Korean. She constantly inquired, "Who is appa?," "Where is appa?" The answer arose, "You should die, then you will see you."

After several failed attempts to kill herself, she made a final resolve. Looking for a place where no one would have to bother with her body, she came to the edge of a cliff on the Han River. But the moment she came to the water, her feet stopped, and she forgot about dying. Sunim stood there for half a day, staring into the water, and finally came to. She walked away. A little time later, she knelt down for a drink from the stream. She saw her exhausted

*The retelling that follows is a paraphrase from *The Inner Path of Freedom: The Teachings of Seon Master Dae Haeng Sunim* (HanMaUm Seon Center, 1999).

face clearly, and wondered why, if her mind felt okay, did her body look so bad. From deep within an answer came, "All is Buddha." The nun saw, for the first time, the true nature of her inner "Appa." From this moment of deep awakening, Sunim went on to be tested by the greatest Zen master of the day. After passing the exam, the master declared her one of the greatest he'd ever met, and she succeeded, for the next forty years, in establishing herself with hundreds of thousands of followers.

I closed the book. My heart was beginning to break open, but my mind raced with judgment. I thought about how, if this woman had been in America, she'd have been involuntarily committed to a state hospital. We simply don't let people walk around crying "Daddy," dirty, hungry and half-naked, trying to throw themselves into rivers. Therefore, she must be truly crazy like my brother, and this biography is just some Zen glorification of insanity, a hagiography in the extreme. Based on that conclusion, I closed my heart and set off for her temple on the outskirts of Seoul.

The meeting in her private quarters was much anticipated by me and the two translators. We walked into a room fit for royalty, with silks, crystal, even a fountain garden; everything was polished and impeccably clean. Senior nuns were fluttering around to make way for the Master. I was anxious, my preconceptions of meeting a Zen master, in addition to someone I thought was probably insane, erupting all at once. Finally, a tiny, old woman came into the room and the nuns came to attention. She had oversized glasses, actually rose-tinted, that matched rosy lips. My preconceptions began melting away. She finally settled onto the couch. Everyone was stiff and formal. She looked right at me, and I suddenly felt about as significant as bellybutton lint, and very self-conscious. I noticed that my being began kind of *voom-vooming*, my whole psyche vibrating at a rate I'd never felt before. I was caught off-guard. As she talked, in Korean, I felt like I understood what she was saying without translation. Her mind seemed to be having a tremendous effect on mine, without my being able to control it at all. After a few polite questions, she gave me the impression that she thought I was being dishonestly intellectual. I finally got down to it. I said, "Would you mind if I ask you something personal?" She nodded. I asked her, "I read your biography. Like you, my own and my brother's childhood saw a lot of trauma in relation to my father. How do we heal this as Buddhists?"

She told me that our mind and our father's mind were the same mind. I felt horrified, even sick, that such a beast would be any part of me. She said that as I transform my mind to forgiveness, compassion, and purity, it would also begin to transform his mind. This wasn't immediately appealing to me. After all, I had worked so many years unentangling the enmeshment and codependency among my brother, our dad, and me. I had worked hard to find a dispassionate distance at which I could hold a person who'd betrayed the trust of a little girl and boy.

Yet by the end of the meeting, I left knowing that I had met with a great being of high realization. I walked away feeling that there could be a great awakening in the face of trauma, perhaps even inspired by trauma. There was hope for someone like my brother. My heart began cracking open. The wall between my brother and me was crumbling.

These days, I look for the qualities and potentialities of the Zen master in my brother. He has an easiness about our parents' misdeeds that I envy. I still fly into rages when they do the stupid things resembling their past. When we go to Mom's for a holiday, everyone is edgy and distant around me but enjoys sitting on the porch shooting the breeze with my brother as he smokes. He listens carefully to the people in his housing development and takes their suffering seriously, respecting the Buddha nature in anyone who comes into his path.

Most of all, I now believe that had it not been for my brother's breakdown, none of the others in my family, including myself, would have been able to begin their paths in healing. Before he became sick, our family was a web of secrets, manipulations, and shame that formed a tight psychic knot no one could untie. I now deeply respect my brother for his unstinting confrontation with suffering and for honestly manifesting the truth of our childhoods, which allowed all of us to loosen that knot. I now understand my brother's difficult years as not simply insanity but as his own meaningful struggle to find freedom.

"Are You Joining a Cult?"

Donna Lovong

"Are you joining a cult?" my mother asked, her eyebrows furrowing. My mom looked anxious as I told her that I would be going to a Buddhist meditation retreat the next weekend. I laughed. "No, Mom, this isn't a cult. Don't you remember what the monks did back when you lived in Laos? I'm doing meditation." She wasn't reassured. Even though our family frequently went to the local Buddhist temple, meditation by laypeople was as foreign to her as offering sticky rice to monks was to me. Mom continued, "Be careful. Don't let them brainwash you." She proceeded to tell me about people at her workplace who followed some kind of group. "I know these Asian women at work who stopped eating meat altogether . . . I think they are being brainwashed."

At first, I couldn't believe that my mother, herself an avowed Buddhist, would think that my meditation practice was weird. I have since come to appreciate the big cultural gap between my mom's Asian past and my American upbringing, and between her ethnic Buddhism and my Western Buddhism. Looking for ways to

Donna Lovong, 26, born in Thailand near the border of Laos, has a BA in sociology and is currently conducting public health research.

bridge our differences, I've probed deeper into my family, my community, and myself.

My parents grew up in Southeast Asia during the 1950s, '60s, and early '70s. In those decades, the region was in constant war and conflict. When the Communist regime expanded into my parents' country in 1975, my mother—pregnant with me at the time—and my father fled and became refugees. We took shelter at a Buddhist temple temporarily, and there I was born. We emigrated to the United States, bringing with us generations of suspicion, mistrust, and anger. I suspect that my parents' experience of being uprooted and of witnessing their own country being "brainwashed" by the Communists is why my mom felt apprehensive when I joined a meditation group.

My mother grew up in a traditional ethnic Chinese family, which had Confucian and Taoist sensibilities mixed in with spirit and nature worship. She told me that no one in her family was Buddhist. She started going to the local Lao Buddhist temple as a teen simply because her friends went there and because the temple taught English classes. She told me that she was drawn to the peaceful grounds of the temple, the sounds of the temple bells, and the chanting of the monks in their colorful robes. My father's side of the family is not Buddhist either. He comes from an ethnic minority group who perform rituals to appease the spirit world. Thus my mother and father were the first ones in their family to partake in Buddhism. Similarly, I am embarking on a path never practiced by any one in my family—a path of Zen meditation and mindfulness practice.

But the Buddhism I grew up with is very different. The Thai and Lao Buddhist temples in the Theravada tradition are centered on community events like Lao and Thai New Year celebrations. Monks performed blessings for a new house or for a sick person. At home, we celebrated Chinese New Year and gave offerings to the spirits of our ancestors at the ancestor altar. My parents and I were never taught meditation. We thought that only monastics meditated and that we laypeople were supposed to earn merit by donating money to the temple, making offerings to the Buddha, and cooking for the monks.

Despite being a Buddhist family, our home was actually filled with anger, violence, and hurtful speech. I remember trying to protect my siblings from my father's uncontrollable rage. The bathroom became our shelter, a place to retreat and find safety. There are many dents and scars in our home, evidence of unskillful actions. Like my father, and his mother before him, I also tried to discipline and control my younger siblings by instilling fear in them. I would be in my room reading alone quietly when I would hear my siblings making a ruckus outside. Instantly, I would lose my patience. I would yell, "Be quiet! Why are you being so loud? You are driving me crazy." I would come out and threaten to beat them if they did not shut up. One time, I lost control and threw a glass at my sister. Another time, I melted my brother's glasses in the microwave.

In high school, I sought ways to control my anger and keep myself sane at home. I asked a teacher how to find quiet time amid the busyness of life. He told me that he dedicated at least ten to fifteen minutes every day to doing nothing. He would sit or lie down in silence and relax, or gaze outside his window and see what was going on outdoors, in the skies and in the yard. He also suggested eating raisins slowly, one at a time, chewing each fifteen to twenty times, while breathing in and out, concentrating on tasting the raisin. I was not aware then that this was my first instruction on mindfulness and meditation—eating meditation, that is.

When I left home for college, I rebelled against my family and its traditions. I didn't want anything to do with the anger and instability of my parents' home, just as I didn't want anything to do with the Buddhist cultural practices of my parents. I felt that my family and my community were just using the Buddhist temple as a filling station. I felt that they partook in the many rituals just to accumulate merit and temporarily relieve their anxieties about life. But afterward, they went right back to their harmful habits of hurting their families, their community, and themselves. People prayed in front of the Buddha for a new car or to win the lottery, as if the Buddha were Santa Claus.

During my college years, I began reading books by Thich Nhat Hanh and Buddhist magazines. I learned about mindfulness, engaged Buddhism, and other Buddhist traditions. I thought to myself, "Wow, there is so much I am not aware of!" I started attending meditation sessions and retreats offered by a local Zen group, comprised of mostly non-Asians. I felt a connection to this group of people who, like me, were all trying to cross over to the other shore of freedom and truth, where lies our true home. I began rediscovering the Buddha, Dharma, and Sangha in a new light, not through my ethnic Buddhist temple, but through Western culture and American Buddhist teachers. I found a Buddhism that spoke to me as a young, Asian-American woman, opening my heart and mind. This path began to heal my wounds; and through mindfulness, I cultivated some sense of patience and compassion.

After eight years away from home, I recently returned to live with my parents. It's a little less chaotic now than when I was growing up, but there are still plenty of times I feel myself really challenged—in a way that living on my own didn't challenge me—to practice compassion, mindfulness, and patience. Still, things feel different. One night, a huge fight broke out between my sister and father. It started because my sister thought that my father was refusing to give her some documents that she needed for school. There was screaming, angry faces and words, hearts racing faster, and misery. An object went flying toward my sister. In that moment, I realized that as much as I tried to stop what was happening, I could not control the situation. I could not control the fear that arose within me. I certainly could not control another human being, whether it was my father, sister, or mother. Although I was scared, I also felt an indescribable sense of calm and stability in letting go of this desire for control.

After my father left the room, I walked past my other sister's room and saw that she was sitting on her bed, her body shaking from listening to the whole incident. When our eyes met, we both started to cry. I knew that this cycle of anger and violence needed to stop, because we were passing this on to younger generations. Somehow I sensed that our own family's cycle had an extended effect on the well-being of the earth itself. I felt our unskillful actions reverberating through the past, present, and future—the consequences going far beyond what we can comprehend.

That night, I urged everyone in the household to practice noble silence (silence of body, speech, and mind) for the rest of the night. I said that unkind words were hurting us all. More than ever, I voiced that we need this quiet time now to calm down and heal and that we must try and refrain from hurting each other further. Amazingly, everyone gave it a try. The next morning, my father gave my sister the documents that she thought he was keeping from her.

Things are getting better at home. The teachings of the Buddha have provided me with the tools to look deeply and understand why my family and I say and do what we do. The study and practice of Buddhism has also helped me to look deeply and understand where my parents are coming from. I am now aware that my anger and hot temper were passed down from my parents and my parents' parents, many generations ago. I feel I am also absorbing the *karma* of my own country's violence and anger, and that of the world.

A few weeks ago, I came home late one night from a long day at work and was starting to prepare dinner for myself. My mom, who was washing dishes, suddenly asked, "When are you going to finish your thesis so that you can get another job that pays more? Hurry up and finish. My friend's son just finished his bachelor's and got a job starting at $60,000. . . ."

In the past, I would have instantly lost my patience and reacted defensively. "Stop getting on my case. I'll finish when I finish. And I've told you before that in my field of work, I won't make that high of a salary." She would respond, "Then why did you pick that field to study? Why didn't you pick doctor or lawyer?" Oh boy, here it goes. We argue some more and then I don't even feel like eating my dinner, so I storm upstairs to my room. These days, though, I'm less bothered by what my mom says. This time around, I responded, "I understand that you want the best for me and our family, but don't worry, I'll finish soon and get another job." I played along and avoided getting excessively involved. Then I said, "OK, I am going to eat dinner now. Let's talk about this another time." I ate peacefully as my seeds of anger didn't arise. These days, I can be patient for much longer periods.

Each day, I learn that all these barriers, problems, negative habits, anger, and jealousies are all part of my path—they are me. They are gifts, too, gifts that provide me with opportunities to practice wholesome ways. For the first time, I feel I am being intimate with my fears by not running away anymore.

My father still asks me occasionally why I meditate. My parents do not understand my meditation practice fully, but they no longer call it a "cult." They seem to have come to some degree of acceptance of my practice. I still participate in the local Lao temple activities, but now I am not blindly following what others are doing.

———————

Just recently, my mother came home from work one evening and asked if I could give her information on meditation places in town. She wanted to give it to her coworker who had inquired about it. Her coworker told her that she had a very good daughter because I practiced meditation. Having someone tell her this altered the way she thought about me and the practice of meditation—I am less odd now. A week later, my mother asked me how she could meditate herself, to calm her mind and be free of worries. The seeds of Dharma are beginning to grow.

Clouds and Water

Jimmy Yu

"Can you do *gongfu?*" I, all of thirteen years old and crazed with martial arts, boldly asked my mom's meditation teacher. Dressed in long brown robes, he was in the middle of a conversation with a lay person after the weekly Sunday meditation. He looked down at me and smiled. "Sure I can," he said. "I can even walk right up this wall, go across the ceiling, and come down the other side, too." My eyes popped open. "This is a cool monk," I thought. He continued, "But if you want to be able to do that, you have to learn meditation first. Come back next Sunday." I came back, again and again, to the Chan center in the middle of Queens, eventually forgetting about gongfu.

In my later teen years, I got heavy into punk and skateboarding, even shaving my head as part of all that. When my mom's master saw my bald head, he smiled and said, "I like your haircut." Privately I retorted, "Yeah, but I shave my head for a different reason." Later, when I was a student in art school, I started doing meditation again, and drew inspirations from Chan for my oil paintings and installations. Because I helped out at the center, I

Jimmy Yu (Guogu), 34, is currently a PhD student in the Department of Religion at Princeton University, with a concentration in Chinese Buddhist history.

was able to participate in seven-day retreats for free. I took full advantage of that, sitting four retreats every year throughout my four years of college. I wanted to become a monk after my first retreat, but my master said that I must wait until I got my bachelor's degree. I also couldn't break up with my longtime girlfriend then. But, just after graduating, I broke up with her, and shaved my head once again. This time it was to ordain as a monk.

I was given what is, perhaps, the most prominent position in the monastic system: the attendant to the Chan master. I had access to *Shifu* (the Chinese honorific for "teacher") whenever I wanted; I was able to observe his every move; I received private teachings and was nurtured like no other person in the center. I also, in accord with the traditional Chinese style of teaching, received a great deal of public humiliation and harsh lessons. Those eight years were intense and difficult, but invaluable. I'm grateful for his lessons which were aimed at wearing away my pride, attachment, and self-centeredness.

I remember one especially challenging incident. The Chan center had bought a new camera so we could take photos of Shifu for PR purposes, such as posters, and we were planning to take shots of him giving his usual Friday night talk. I began setting up the camera behind the crowd. The hall was packed that night and everyone was excited. We had arranged another translator so I would be able to take the shots. Just before he began his talk, Shifu said to the crowd in English, "Look at him, faking to be a professional! He can't possibly take photographs . . . he's no good." Shifu laughed and the crowd joined in with him. Everyone was laughing at me except the resident monks. They looked sorry for me, especially my senior brother monk Guochou. Though the "joke" started the lecture off on a fun note, I felt cut by his words. I sat there and looked at Shifu, speechless, from the back of the room. I got up and walked out. No photos were taken that night.

*The Chinese honorific for teacher.

Sitting in my room, first in tears, then in rage, I began punching my pillow. "That's it. I'm fed up with that old man!" I began packing my belongings. Guochou came in and began trying to talk me into staying. We spoke for a long time. Guochou tried to draw an analogy between my situation and that of the Tibetan medieval master Milarepa. He also talked about how Shifu was following the same method of training that he himself had received from his master. "I don't think Shifu's training me," I said. "I think he's just being an asshole!"

Nevertheless, I stayed. I didn't speak to Shifu for three days. I remember Shifu used to say that "in the old days" good attendants received harsh treatments from their masters and would not be scared away or discouraged. He would tell me that there's a saying in the Chan tradition: good disciples are born out of the end of the stick, the instrument used in the Chan Hall to strike meditators. I would think to myself, "Yes, but I grew up in America! We don't believe in old Chinese methods for treating disciples. We believe that a person grows through encouragement and support." Now I see my reactions as partly an excuse arising from my wounded pride.

My relationship with Shifu was complex. Despite his training method—"training through adversities," as he would say—he was actually a compassionate man and in many ways treated me like his own son. I remember our first Dharma-teaching trip abroad. We had been invited by a kind, Czech-born monk to the Czech Republic. Shifu and I stayed at a beautiful village hotel. We even had our own kitchen. While at the home monastery he had other attendants cook for him, here, as his attendant, I would need to take care of everything.

For our first meal, Shift asked if I knew how to cook. "Sure," I replied confidently. Actually, I only knew how to cook egg-fried rice—and monks do not eat eggs! "Improvise, improvise....

Think! Lunch time is near," I thought to myself. I rushed out to the local market for groceries. The market had little except some cabbage, tomatoes, and piles of meat. I gathered the vegetables and rushed back to our hotel to start the adventure. "Let's see. Shifu has a bad stomach and his palette is light. I'll just cook him a soup with everything in it!" I waited until the water boiled and threw everything in. "Add a dash of salt and we're good to go."

You should have seen the look on his face when he took the first sip of soup. I started to get a bad feeling about what would come next. "This is just water and vegetables! I thought you said you could cook," Shifu said. I was silent, preparing to be yelled at. I thought to myself, "I'm only a novice . . . what did you expect?" Shifu looked at me, sighed, and said, "Looks like I'll have to teach you how to cook as well." He smiled with pity. "Sorry, Shifu!" I said, feeling like a burden.

As it turned out, he was very excited to be cooking again. He told me how he learned to cook when he lived in Japan; I watched and absorbed his techniques wholeheartedly. We had a good time in the kitchen. From then on, I was able to use the principles of what he taught me to create many more dishes. Thanks to him, a couple of years from then, I had the honor of serving breakfast to our entire *sangha* at our home monastery in Taiwan. After that, fortunately for Shifu, I was able to serve him better food whenever we traveled abroad.

Traveling with Shifu, shuttling every three months between the monastery in Taiwan and the center in Queens, I had many opportunities to receive other "extemporaneous teachings." Shifu was quick to nail me down and point out my attachments. I remember one time sitting in the car with him, driving towards the airport. Not long after we left the home monastery, still thinking about what a great time I had in Taiwan, I said, "Shifu, when will we return again? Next time I return, I want to...."

"*Uuhh!*" Shifu retorted in a loud, impatient voice. "What are you saying? Who knows where you'll be in the future?! Monks travel like clouds and water. Don't you plan about what you want to do in the future! Wherever you are, you should be able to be content."

I sat there silently and I bowed to him in my heart. I knew he was right. I had grown attached to the home monastery in Taiwan, my fellow brothers and sisters, and the lifestyle. Instead of being like "clouds and water," an expression for traveling monks, my attachments were more like rocks and mountains. I realized that as a monk the path I'd chosen was a path of solitude and freedom. Like clouds and water, the life of a monk should be free flowing, without obstructions, and never leaving traces like hang-ups and social ties. This was the meaning of leaving home, yet, with all of my clinging and passions, I was so far from actualizing it. Shifu had once again brought me back to the present, reminding me of my practice. The rest of the ride to the airport was silent. Shifu returned to resting. Like clouds and water, he left no traces of what had just happened. The driver monk was familiar with this scene, where I was scolded again, and was quiet himself. I sat there quietly too, just being open and aware of the cushion in the back seat I was sitting on, the window, the rice fields on the side of the highway, and my breath.

Early in my career as Shifu's attendant monk, he called me "the boy." In Chinese the word *xiao haizi* connotes someone immature and naive, with an implication of absent-mindedness. He knew how much it would get to me whenever he called me, "Hey boy!" It was the quickest way to shoot down my ego, especially in public and at the age when I thought I was already a "grown man." I remember one day, he said to me after the evening service in front of the assembly, "Hey boy, you chant the four great vows pretty good." I smiled, because I was always proud of my chanting. Then he said, "How are you going to 'deliver all sentient beings' if you can't even remember the things that *one* sentient being needs? If you can learn to take care of one sentient being—me, your Shifu—in the future you will know how to take care of a sangha. If you know how to take care of the whole sangha, you will know how to take care of other beings, then all sentient beings. Don't forget this, and the needs of others." He turned around and left the hall along with the assembly.

The service was over, and I stood there alone, still in the main Dharma hall. Feeling ashamed, I rushed to Shifu's quarters in tears and prostrated to him. "Shifu, I will never forget anything you need. I mean, I will try my best not to forget anything anymore!" He didn't say much except, "We'll see." Of course, I still forgot stuff now and then. I was absent-minded partly because I was young, but I also realized that the cause of absent-mindedness was self-centeredness. Knowing this, I trained myself to always try to put others before myself. Whenever I met another person, I would think, "What can I offer this person?" For me, the "letting go" of the self, in practice, became offering myself. I combined this with advice from Shifu to "use the body like a rag; use your mind like a mirror."

Over the years, Shifu eased up on the humiliation method of training me—at least, he used it only on rare occasions. My responsibilities had shifted from being an attendant to assisting him in teaching his students. I would like to think that he felt I didn't need lessons as often, but the real reason is that one time I actually left the monastery, without permission, to see what was out there. He saw this as a sign that I would soon leave permanently. It wasn't until later that I heard from my fellow monks and lay members how sad Shifu was about my leaving.

After more than three months on my own, I returned, hoping to see a change in the way the center was ran. Things hadn't changed. I decided it was time to leave. I expressed to Shifu my desire to go to graduate school for Buddhist studies. He agreed hesitantly, but predicted that once I left, I may not stay a monk anymore. I remember the sadness in his eyes as we parted.

Many things had built up to a point where it was time for me to leave: the increasing burden of my temple responsibilities, my frustration with the institutionalization and bureaucracy of the organization, and my need to find a way to grow up and really be my own person. But all these hinged on my relationship with Shifu. I began understanding the impact of my not really having had a father and growing up in a dysfunctional family. Although my intellectual and spiritual sides had developed as a monk, emotionally a side of me was still like a boy seeking affection. This manifested as projections onto Shifu as my father, and in the eventual schism I had with him (excuses, really) in my last year as a monk. In leaving, I hoped to take time away from Shifu and to grow emotionally.

I spent several years out in the world, studying, working, and soaking up complex experiences from life: love, separation, joy, aloneness, and death of those close to me. In the midst of these experiences, as Shifu had predicted, I did disrobe. But these valuable experiences brought home Shifu's lessons in ways that, curiously, I would have never learned within the walls of his monastery.

Now that I live closer to New York, I regularly visit the Chan center in Queens, still translating for Shifu from time to time, or just listening delightedly when the old man gives talks. Recently, after one of his talks, Shifu asked if anyone had questions. People in the audience asked about this and that, but questions steered into politics. Shifu responded only generally, but people pressed on. Sitting in the back of the room, I raised my hand. Shifu saw me and said, "Ah, Guogu's here!" People turned their heads. I stood up and expressed my opinion that Shifu, being a monk, should not have to answer specific political questions or take sides, but only to provide principles in the Dharma for practitioners in the world. Shifu smiled and said, "Thank you for saving me!" and started laughing. Everyone joined in. The room lightened up. Then he asked, "What do you think about my earlier talk?" I responded directly, pointing out what I thought was good and the areas that need clarification. Our rapport and repartee surprised people. He thought for a moment, nodded, and said, "Very good. Let's talk more about this later."

Longtime Buddhists

When I Was Young, No One Had Plans

ZOKETSU NORMAN FISCHER

I have a theory that religious practitioners are born, not made. And that probably everyone has a religious practitioner deep inside. I also think all children make vows from an early age to practice deep living, total goodness, truth, growth, and compassion. But as they grow up and have to socialize themselves—to be someone in a world full of other someones—they forget about this. They literally forget. Then maybe something happens to them later on in life that causes them to remember.

Like all good theories, this one comes from my own experience. When I was quite young—maybe four or five—I was a strange kid. Lonely and brooding. I did not consider myself strange, of course, but I could tell I must have been strange because my parents seemed worried about me. I could also tell that I was different from other children. I used to spend long hours looking out the window of our small apartment that was located over my grandparents' tailor shop. The scene outside looked like a 1940s film noir movie: a small, dark, quiet city street, with an occasional car passing by. It

Zoketsu Norman Fischer, 56, *a Zen priest and poet, and former abbot of the San Francisco Zen Center, recently published* Taking Our Places: The Buddhist Path to Truly Growing Up.

made you think about life, about death, about the strangeness of time. The cars made a sad swooshing sound in the quiet night. Where were they going? And why? What did it all amount to? These were the kinds of things I thought about. I wanted to know the answers to these questions. I suppose that is a little strange for a five-year-old.

My family was Jewish and we belonged to a Conservative synagogue. It was a small synagogue, but there were services every day and I often attended them. I can remember walking to services with my father, him holding my small hand in his big hand, him so tall (though actually my father was not a tall man) and me so short. I remember how immense the sidewalk seemed as we walked on it—and that it had mica or something in it that made it sparkle in the streetlights.

I liked going to temple. There were a lot of old men there, immigrants from Europe, who would say their prayers with fervor, swaying as they prayed in a blissed-out trance state, surrounded by a quiet wrapped around them like the prayer shawls they wore. I took this devotion and spiritual focus for granted and didn't think about it (though I think it was one of the reasons I liked to go to temple). It is only now I recognize that these men must have been truly spiritual people. They are long dead, and I doubt there are any more like them.

The rabbi in our town at that time was a wonderful lively young man named Gabriel Maza. He was the brother of the famous comedian Jackie Mason, who is, incidentally, also a rabbi. Like his brother, Rabbi Maza was funny and witty and had a deep religious faith to match his intellectual brightness. Bored in our small town, where no one in the congregation was educated or interested in religious matters, he was looking for someone to talk to. That turned out to be me. From the age of about eleven on, I studied with the Rabbi in a private class, just the two of us. We studied everything—not only Torah and Talmud, but philosophy, literature, all sorts of things. I remember very little of those things now, but I will never forget the wonderful feeling of serious study, and of discussion, and of how delightful it can be to spend time thinking about life and God and what is real.

By the time I entered high school Rabbi Maza had left our town to be closer to New York, where he was from. At the same time, my life was changing drastically. I stopped looking out the window at the cars. There was no more reading religious books or going to temple. Instead life was full of sports, girls, social life. The world outside our town started to come to life for me. I wanted to know more about it, to see and explore it. I wanted to be a writer, and had already started, at about the age of twelve, to write stories and poems. I went away to college with that in mind.

During my high school years I felt as if I were becoming a different person, quite distinct from who I had been when I was younger. I had been shy, brooding, withdrawn. Now I was outgoing, confident, social. I have no idea how this shift happened, but it did. I had a great time in high school; life was full, and the prospects for the future were immense. But when I went to college I seemed to revert to my childhood persona. I'm not sure why. Maybe it was because the college was full of people who came from large cities and were competitive and worldly. Maybe it was the weather and the place—northern New York state, cold in winter, dark and bleak from November till May. Whatever it was, being in college reminded me of something bleak and sad inside myself that I had set aside from my childhood. I wasn't expecting it to come back and when it did, it really threw me.

This was also the time of the Vietnam War, which had two effects on me, as on many other young men my age. First, it shocked me into the realization that my country and its government were not to be believed and trusted, as I had always assumed, and second, I was now in the very real danger of getting called to the army, of having to fight and maybe die for this untrustworthy government and its policies. As a young man who wanted to be a writer I felt that I should go to war and fight—then come home and write a novel about it. This is what so many young men had done after World War II; these were the novels I read as a young man. But, on the other hand, the more I thought about it the more I could see it would be impossible for me to fight in an unjust cause. I became an anti-war activist. This was also a time, as everyone knows, when marijuana and other psychedelic drugs were introduced to the society at large. I took them and they also contributed to the feeling I had that the world was turning upside down. Within a few years I was a hippie dropout, burned out on anti-war activism, still wanting to write and read books, but alienated fairly thoroughly from the society in which I lived. The last thing in the world that I could see myself doing was joining society, getting a job or a profession. All I wanted to do was be by myself and heal my wounds.

When I was in college, my return to brooding and thinking had led me to study religion. I encountered the writings of D. T. Suzuki, one of the first Asians to write about Japanese Zen in English for an educated Western audience. Suzuki's books made Zen seem the best possible way to look at life. With all the Buddhist centers now established in the United States and Europe it seems hard to believe that in those days Buddhism was more or less unknown in the West. There were no centers at all. Buddhism was something you read about in a book, something archaic or exotic. And Suzuki's books seemed to corroborate this idea. Even though it is impossible now to think of Zen without thinking of Zen meditation, somehow Suzuki seemed hardly to mention it. He spoke about *koans,* the stories of the old teachers, and had many important theoretical things to say about mind and enlightenment and the unconscious. But he gave the impression that Zen was the *idea* of Zen. It was only later, when I met someone who had been an early student of the San Francisco Zen Center, that I realized there was a practice a person could do to actively seek enlightenment. As soon as I heard about the Zen Center I decided to go there. In 1970 I moved to California with the idea of learning how to do Zen meditation and then going to live by myself in the woods, to meditate, study, hike, and write books.

That's what I did for about three years. I had no interest in hanging around the Zen Center or getting to know people. I wasn't looking for community—I wanted to be left alone. I didn't want to find a teacher—I was too stubborn for that. Besides, I didn't know you were supposed to have a teacher. I would go to lectures when from time to time I came to the Bay Area from one of my many cabins in northern California (I moved around a lot), but I'd leave as soon as the lecture was over. All I wanted to do was meditate and write and be quiet. It was a wonderful if lonely life while it lasted. I'd go on long walks, spend days and weeks at a time not talking to anyone. Sometimes I'd go off into the Sierra mountains for a week or two, fishing for food and sleeping beside alpine lakes.

After a while I ran out of money and also realized that I needed to learn more about meditation practice and to sit with others. I moved to Berkeley and joined the Berkeley Zen Center, where I had first learned how to sit. Sojun Mel Weitsman, who was and still is the head priest there, became my first Zen teacher. His style of teaching, inherited from his teacher Suzuki Roshi, was very simple. It was just to sit faithfully every day, to tend the garden and cook the meals. Since this was how I was living anyway, it appealed to me a great deal. There was no fanfare or complication. The Berkeley Zen Center was small and simple. The *zendo* was in the attic of an old Berkeley house, and there were just a few of us sitting every day in the early mornings. Looking back on it now, I see it was a very pure and innocent practice. We just lived our lives and meditated. I spent my days as a student in religious studies at the Graduate Theological Union in Berkeley. Later, after I finished my degree there, I started a small gardening business.

While I was still studying Zen with Sojun in Berkeley I started going to the Zen Center in San Francisco to hear Baker Roshi (Suzuki Roshi's successor) give Dharma talks. While I didn't much like the Zen Center (it was so big, and so official, and people seemed so serious and pious) I did enjoy Baker Roshi's talks. They were complicated, rambling, full of social and cultural references—and all of that appealed to me.

In the summer of 1971 or '72, I made a visit to the Zen Center monastery at Tassajara Hot Springs, in Los Padres National Forest. I took to it immediately. It was the stones that did it—immense boulders that had been deposited there millennia ago by glaciers, and smoothed over through the ages by the rushing waters of Tassajara Creek. The monastery grounds were full of them. They were constantly being hauled around for the many building projects that were going on then—a new kitchen was under construction, and many stone walls and pathways were going up. The hot mountain sun beating down on those boulders seemed to ring inside me like the huge temple bell that was struck for meditation in the early morning, evening, and at night before bed. The immense quiet of the place appealed strongly to something inside me. I knew that one way or the other, and no matter what it took, I would go there and stay as long as I could. I went home and started saving money.

Meanwhile, I met the woman who would soon become my wife, and she and I decided to go to Tassajara together, which we did within a few years. But we could only stay for one ninety-day training period, because she was by then already pregnant with our twin sons. We left Tassajara for the birth, but when our sons were about six months old we returned, and stayed there continuously until they were five years old and ready to go to school.

Tassajara was and still is a wonderful place to practice. Deep in the mountains, very far from any other human habitation, and without radio, television, or newspapers—there isn't even any electricity or heat! Tassajara monks live the traditional Zen monastic schedule, which started in those days at about 3:30 A.M. There were a few hours a day for work and bathing, but otherwise all waking hours were spent in contemplation and meditation. It was a great life, full of many inner wonders. Kathie and I loved it even though the life wasn't easy. The children loved it, too, and look back with pride and wonder at their odd upbringing.

Recently, one of our sons came home and we got to talking. "What was your plan in those days?" he asked me. It was impossible to explain to him that in those days you didn't *have a plan.* You just did what you believed in for as long as you believed in it, and expected that whatever was supposed to happen next simply would. I had no interest in becoming a lifetime resident of Zen Center, or of ordaining as a Zen priest. I just wanted to stay at Tassajara as long as I could, carrying out my original impulse. I had no plan beyond that. After a while, though, Baker Roshi told me that if I wanted to continue to stay at Tassajara on scholarship (after about the first year Kathie and I ran out of funds) I had better make my serious intentions clear by ordaining as a priest. This was a crisis for me because I did not want to become a Zen priest—I was a poet, not a priest!—but neither was I ready to leave the monastery. So I decided to ordain—and Kathie ordained with me. Our sons, about three years old at the time, had a giggling fit when they first saw us with our smoothly shaven heads.

Kathie's parents were amazingly tolerant of our choice to become Zen Buddhist monks. I can't say why—only that they seemed to feel the Zen Center was a reasonable organization, and that we were intelligent people who knew what we were doing. They may or may not have been right on both counts. My own parents, on the other hand, who had remained all their lives in a small Pennsylvania town, had a much harder time with it. My mother died too young, still hoping that somehow I would reform and become the lawyer or doctor she had always expected. After she died my father came to visit us a lot and learned to accept our Zen life. He couldn't understand it, but he could see we were happy, had a place to live and food to eat, and that our children were well. I think he could also see that I had improved as a person through my practice. I was kinder and less unreasonable, and he and I made a good relationship together, after fighting almost continuously since my adolescence.

When Kathie and I left Tassajara in 1981, we moved to Green Gulch Farm temple north of San Francisco, intending to stay for just a few years. But somehow it rapidly became about twenty years. There were always things to do. For some years I worked on the organic farm, then was director of Green Gulch, treasurer, head of the meditation hall, head teacher, and in 1995 I became co-abbot of Zen Center. Throughout my time at Zen Center I had great advantages: I could practice Zen every day as part of my job and take classes. Since the center is so large and famous, it has hosted many visiting teachers over the years, like Thich Nhat Hanh and the Dalai Lama, and so I had the benefit of meeting and studying with many teachers from many traditions. Zen Center's various troubles and organizational difficulties—most notably the famous scandal and split with Baker Roshi—I found also to be valuable lessons for me. Seeing all this stuff go down over a thirty-year period or so has shown me the other side of Buddhism's pure idealistic teachings—the realistic side of what people actually do with the practice over time. How it works and doesn't work. All the ways you can go wrong, right, and half-wrong and half-right. It's been a great education.

Now I have started a small organization of my own, the Everyday Zen Foundation, where I can practice again simply, with just a few friends and students. I travel a lot, and seem to be able to earn enough to live on just the donations I receive for teaching. I see now, and saw consistently over the years at Zen Center, how relevant and important some serious Buddhist practice can be for establishing a firm ethical and spiritual foundation for a lifetime. Whether or not you want to be a Buddhist—or spend any significant amount of time in your life as a Buddhist student—it is still worthwhile to practice seriously when you are young. So many people run around getting credentials and skills for living in the world. Of course this is important and practical. Nowadays you do need a plan. But if you don't know why you are alive and how you need to live inside, all the credentials and skills in the world are irrelevant. They will never get you where you really want to go. Outer development without inner development is insufficient. But if you establish a strong spiritual basis then you will surely find what you need in this lifetime. Whatever else you need to learn you will learn. At least this has been my experience so far— not only with myself but with the thousands of other people I have worked with and seen over the years.

Full Circle

KATHLEEN MILLANE OLESKY

Eileen scoffed, "What's this? Your latest craze?"

My face grew hot. I tried to control my voice in the face of my sister's ridicule. "Look," I said, "I don't understand much about what I'm doing right now. You can laugh all you want. I can't explain it, but I think I'm going to do this for the rest of my life." She looked at me in surprise. Even I was taken aback by my own passionate declaration.

It was April 1973. I was twenty years old, a transfer student at Hampshire College, and I had begun my practice of Buddhism. I was home for the weekend to receive the *Gohonzon,* the scroll that marked the beginning of my practice. My sister walked in on me as I was trying to recite the strange words from a little blue book. I didn't blame her for her skepticism; I hadn't been a model of stability. I was a quitter. Drugs, anti-war protests, and the hippie movement had claimed me—I attended three colleges in three years. Now I was going to be a Buddhist for life? This is how it happened.

Kathleen Millane Olesky, 51, a student of Nichiren Buddhism, has been a regional leader for the New England organization for many years.

Three days before the campus emptied for Spring Break, I went to a Herbie Hancock concert at Amherst College. Three days later I hitchhiked to New York with a friend. After a few adventurous rides, a kindly truck driver deposited us safely in midtown Manhattan around 2:00 A.M. We crashed at a friend's apartment on the Upper West Side. The next day, we set off to help a friend film a movie. Michael had made lots of friends in the film industry through his dad and he was working on an art film. We headed over to an apartment on Riverside Drive. When we got there, a name on the mailbox jumped out at me: *H. Hancock* was neatly written above the bell.

"H. Hancock!" I exclaimed. "That doesn't stand for Herbie Hancock by any chance? Not *the* Herbie Hancock?!"

"It sure does. Didn't I tell you he lived here? But don't get too excited," said Michael. "He moved to LA a few months ago. He sublets this place to a couple of guys."

I tried to conceal my disappointment and followed Michael into the building. The subletting friends were engaged in filming each other sitting around the kitchen table. I was introduced to the assortment of amateur filmmakers. Then I proceeded to make myself inconspicuous, exploring my surroundings.

About a half-hour later, the hall door opened and in walked the jazz musician himself. The filmmakers came out of the kitchen and greeted Herbie casually.

I stood frozen in the doorway of the living room. I tried to appear calm, as if bumping into famous jazz musicians was an everyday occurrence.

He walked up to me and held out his hand.

"Hi," I croaked. My mouth was so dry. "I just saw you in Amherst the other day—Wednesday, I think it was."

"Oh," he smiled. He had a casual, humble way about him, not in the least like a famous jazz musician. "What a strange coincidence."

The smiled broadened and he looked momentarily mysterious. "Would you like to come to a meeting?"

"Yeah, sure," I said. I didn't even ask what kind of a meeting. Before I knew it, Michael, myself, someone who turned out to be Herbie's cousin, Gil, and another woman named Hazel were piling into Herbie's station wagon, driving across town. I was sitting in the front seat, squeezed in between Herbie and Michael and feeling awkward. Then I realized the conversation seemed to be about Buddhism. Slowly, it began to dawn on me that he was taking us to a Buddhist meeting! I was horrified! When I thought of Buddhism, I envisioned the Hare Krishnas: men with topknots and saffron robes, dancing, beating drums, and chanting.

How did I get into this? I thought, as we pulled up in front of a low rise on Fifteenth Street. As we made our way up to the second floor, the air sounded like it was buzzing with a thousand bees. We entered a huge studio with about two hundred people sitting on the floor, reciting indecipherable words. I was immediately struck by the variety of people: white, black, Asian, Latino, Irish, Italian, old people, middle-aged people, and children. Some appeared wealthy, others more blue-collar. I couldn't find the common denominator of this group, except for the fact that they were all saying the same words and facing a wooden box on the wall that had a white scroll inscribed with Chinese characters.

Kneeling next to me, Herbie pointed to the words written in a little blue book. His finger pointed to each syllable on the paper. *Nam-myoho-renge-kyo.* I resisted saying them. My throat felt as if it had closed. I was suddenly self-conscious, embarrassed by the sound of my own voice.

A gong sounded and the chanting stopped abruptly. Everybody got up and started running around the room, gathering into groups. Some brought out musical instruments, others began warm-up exercises and others started singing scales. *What a strange form of Buddhism,* I thought. Herbie said the people were rehearsing for an upcoming musical show. It was very confusing. But most confusing of all was that these extremely different people seemed to like each other. There was marked absence of tension that one would expect from such a range of people. Everyone was laughing and talking; it was as if they shared a secret I didn't understand. I was suspicious of their obvious happiness, an emotion quite foreign to me.

I ended up spending that whole evening with Herbie. After the meeting, we went to visit his friend Dolores.

"Come in, come in!" Dolores said. "Make yourselves at home. Lordy! You never know what's gonna happen when Herbie comes to town."

Dolores pointed to a box that was hanging on the wall of her living room. She opened it and inside was the same scroll I had seen earlier.

"This here," she said in a matter-of-fact voice, "is my Gohonzon. It represents my Buddha nature, the pattern of my enlightenment, and when I chant to it, my enlightened self starts to come out." She said this with such assurance, in such a no-nonsense manner, that I believed her. Why would this woman lie to me?

Everyone knelt down in front of the scroll. Dolores pulled out a little blue book and showed me each syllable with her finger." *Myoho renge kyo. Hoben-pon dai ni. Niji seson ju sanmai anjo niki go...*." This went on for twenty minutes. My knees ached, my feet fell asleep and I was very restless. I got up and wandered over to the full-length window that overlooked Central Park. It was surreal.

During dinner, Dolores and Herbie talked about Buddhism and how this practice had affected their lives.

"You know," Dolores said. "Whenever I get down or stressed, I just sit down and chant these words, and before I know it I am feeling better."

Herbie explained, "These words: *Nam-myoho-renge-kyo* (the *daimoku*) are like a rhythm, a vibration that permeates everything in the universe, so when you say them, it's like you're harmonizing and fusing with this ultimate law of cause and effect and manifest enlightenment." He then told me that since he had begun chanting, he had been able to make great advancement in his music. It was important to have a particular goal in mind when reciting the words, to focus on a particular problem. The practice involved reciting the *sutra,* the little book, and chanting the daimoku twice a day, morning and evening. "Enlightenment really means to unite yourself with the rhythm of the universe so you can live with freedom and joy, no matter what happens."

We asked questions. Michael was quite skeptical. But something told me to sit up and pay attention, that this was a crucial moment in my life. Dolores was down to earth, genuine and embracing. She won me over completely. We talked and laughed until four in the morning. It's not the words we spoke that I remember most, it is the sensation of that night in New York that has stayed with me over the years. I felt that I had known these people for centuries. Dolores' apartment on Central Park West was a place of enchantment and I had arrived there for a reason. I was soothed, energized, and felt connected to something I didn't quite understand.

I attended several Buddhist meetings in Boston. The people had that same immediate warmth as the ones I had seen in New York. Every time I went to a meeting, I had the feeling I had met these people before. People at the meeting encouraged me to chant.

"Chant for anything you want," they said. Chanting for things seemed crass but I tried it. I chanted for Herbie Hancock to call me. He did. I wasn't home.

A month after meeting Dolores and Herbie, I received my own scroll, the Gohonzon, at a ceremony in Boston. I hitchhiked back to Amherst, clutching my scroll. I was told some local members would come and help me enshrine it. A few days later, two petite Japanese women appeared at my dorm room. They introduced themselves as Akiko and Tomoko. I hurried them inside, checking the hallway in hopes that none of my dorm-mates were around. If the ladies noticed my discomfort, they didn't let on. They set about cheerfully unpacking the items for my altar: an incense burner, a box of incense, candleholder, and two candles.

Akiko looked around the room. "Now, Kathy-san, where do we put Gohonzon?"

"I don't know," I said. "I don't have anything to put it in." *Where the hell I am supposed to put an altar in this box of a room?* I thought.

Meanwhile, Tomoko was pulling out the drawers of my desk. "Look here," she said as she pulled the bottom drawer all the way out. "We can use this." She handed me a stack of papers from the drawer, stood the drawer on its side and exclaimed, "Perfect!" She placed the drawer on top of a chest. We knelt together while Akiko unrolled the scroll and hung it on a thumbtack inside the drawer. We chanted to my pathetic, makeshift altar. Tomoko took a silk scarf from her bag and draped it over the front of the drawer. "To protect it from dust," she said.

"Now, Kathy-san. You all set. Chant everyday. Come to meetings. Teach your friends to chant! Bye-bye."

They left as quickly as they had appeared. I watched them bustle down the hall, giggling in Japanese. The big guy who lived in the room next to mine almost knocked them down coming out of his room. He looked surprised. I ducked back in my room before he saw me.

Pretty soon, enthusiasm for my newfound spirituality flagged. I could only chant late at night since I was too tired in the mornings. With no one to consistently teach me the words in the little book, I skipped a lot. The magic of that night in New York began to fade. I began to think that the whole thing was a hoax. Of course Herbie Hancock was happy. He was a wealthy, successful jazz musician and I was just a screwed-up transfer student without a clue as to where I was going. I felt duped.

Just when I was about to quit entirely, I got a call from another member who invited me to a local Buddhist meeting that was held on Thursdays at nearby Westover Airforce Base. The next Thursday night, I stuck my thumb out on Route 16 and got a ride to the house of Bill and Akiko Simonette. Bill was an Air Force retiree and his wife, Akiko, turned out to be the same woman who came to enshrine my scroll. They welcomed me into their humble home as if I were their own daughter and I liked them immediately. After we ate, we drove to the meeting. I could not fathom where their genuineness came from. From the time I got in their car until we reached the security gate, I did nothing but complain about how chanting did not work. Bill and Akiko just laughed and said, "Don't worry, keep at it, don't give up."

I don't quite understand why I kept going back to these Buddhist meetings on an Air Force base. It was quite a bizarre scene, me with my Moroccan robe, bell-bottoms, and long flowing red hair kneeling together with a room full of service men and their impeccably groomed Japanese wives. During the discussion part of the meetings, I usually sat in the corner, sullen and critical of these warm and generous people who seemed happier than anyone I had ever seen. Despite my skepticism and discomfort, I continued to practice.

As I continued my practice, it became more difficult to run away from my problems with drugs or trips on weekends, or to put off doing my schoolwork. Usually, if I were having a bad week, I would go to New York or Boston. Whenever offered the opportunity to flee, I was gone regardless of studies. But there was another, less familiar voice emerging within me, a higher self who tried to beat out my weaker side. Once, while I was packing for one of my weekend getaways, I was wracked with conflict about whether to go or stay and write a term paper.

The escapist in me won; she was still stronger. But I had a terrible time in New York. I regretted not staying on campus and writing the paper. I suspected this inner conflict might have something to do with that Buddhist chanting. I was annoyed. If this Buddhism was about becoming a better, more responsible person, then I wasn't ready.

The first year of my practice was rocky. I was still plagued by anxiety, indecision, and depression. Finally, I received advice from a senior member. He told me to concentrate on small, immediate goals that involved helping others. He could see that I was lost in the quagmire of my own problems so he suggested that I stopped thinking about my own situation for a while to chant specifically about other people. Desperate, I decided to follow his advice. Whenever I chanted, I thought only of achieving my short-term goal of carrying out compassionate acts on behalf of others. Strangely, even though I wasn't chanting about myself, I was happier and more confident.

Over the past thirty years, my practice of Nichiren Buddhism has helped me transform countless sufferings and fulfill many personal goals. One of the biggest tests came when my boyfriend dumped me during my second year of practice. Previously, I would fall into months of deep depression as the result of a broken heart. This time, I prayed to change poison into medicine. After three hours of chanting and summoning up the strength to continue in my life, I emerged happier and healthier than I had been in the relationship. The struggle to transform heartache convinced me of one true thing: I was solely in control of my happiness and no one—lover, parent, or friend—could give it to me. Nor could they take it away. Strangely, six months later this same man came back into my life. We have been married for twenty-seven years and have three extraordinary children.

Last year my eighteen-year-old son, George, struggled through the year of college applications. I chanted many hours for his success during this grueling process. He ultimately chose Hampshire College, the school I left just as I had begun my practice. In late August, we brought him up to college and moved him into his dormitory. Before we left him, he asked if we could chant together. He opened his small scroll and we knelt before it to recite the Lotus Sutra. As we chanted, the sound of our rhythmical daimoku filling the room, tears flowed down my cheeks. I realized I had come full circle.

The Long and Winding Road

LAMA SURYA DAS

Who knows where our spiritual life begins, it is hard to say, but gradually it becomes clearer and clearer. When I was a teenager, I never knew what was going on but I certainly was trying damn hard to find out. I still don't know what's going on, but now it bothers me less. I met Buddhism when I was seventeen. I was in college at the University of Buffalo. It was the "Roaring Sixties"— a good time.

My roommate David and I hitchhiked to Rochester in November of our freshman year to go on a Buddhist meditation retreat. A psychology professor whose encounter groups we had been participating in had invited us to this Zen weekend retreat at Philip Kapleau's Rochester Zen Center, one of the first Zen centers in America. I found it was very hard to sit *zazen*. Some of the forty-five minute silent meditations seemed interminable. The teacher went around and prodded students with a little stick to keep them awake and alert. I was very impressed by the roshi's clarity and kindness.

Lama Surya Das, 51, is the founder of the Dzogchen Foundation, and author of Awakening the Buddha Within.

The discipline helped clear my mind and concentrate my ener-
gies. It was hard but doable. That lesson has become clear to me
over the years: it is hard to transform, it is hard to wake up, it is
hard to grow up, hard to become a *mensch*. But it is doable, and it
is necessary. One can get used to hard practice. Being pushed by a
legitimate teacher, healthy discipline is a great way to transcend
one's own mind-made limits and ego resistance.

After that weekend, I was sure that I would go back to my dormitory and meditate for half an hour every day like a good little
Buddha should. I might have made it to Monday with that vow,
but by Tuesday other matters intruded. Classes, late night activities, rock concerts, and political activism took over. I was looking
into lots of new things, still searching for *something*. Meanwhile,
events like the Vietnam War were overtaking us. Truth be told, the
smoke in my dormitory was too thick to meditate.

I began reading about Buddhism, Hinduism, and Eastern philosophy, and thinking about how that compared with Western philosophy. Philosophers like Schoepenhauer, Nietzsche, Wittgen-
stein, and existentialists like Camus spoke to me about reality, but
Eastern thought was luring me. Then I was turned on to Alan Watts,
R. D. Lang, Ram Dass, Aldous Huxley, Kurt Vonnegut, and Her-
mann Hesse. I was on fire at the time, spiritually speaking, to figure
things out.

Before I knew it, I was a junior. My best friend's girlfriend, Alli-
son Krause, was shot and killed demonstrating at Kent State, May
4, 1970. You may have heard CSNY's song about it. She was one of
the four students shot and killed by the National Guard while
protesting Nixon and Kissinger's secret bombings of Cambodia.
That turned my head around about radical politics. I started to
think about the contradictions inherent in *fighting* for peace. I
wanted to find inner peace and make peace with these tragic
events and shocking personal experiences. That was a big wakeup

call for baby-boomer boy—me—happy-go-lucky Jeffrey Miller, Long Island jock.

Interestingly enough, karmic connections appeared. Another one of those four who got shot that day was also named Jeffrey Miller, also a Kent State student from Long Island. That night my parents and my brother thought that it was me who had been shot (until they heard from me by phone). There is a cover of *Time* magazine of a teenage runaway girl kneeling and grieving over a bloody, dead boy—identified as Jeffrey Miller. That turned my head around, too. I started to get disillusioned with fighting for peace and radical politics. I questioned whether our protests really had any effect, although I suppose the peace movement did contribute to the end of that terrible, wasteful conflict, the Vietnam War.

I graduated from college with honors and a fellowship to graduate school. On graduation day I got on a flight and headed off toward India—not that I knew exactly what I was doing.

I traveled across Europe, the Near East, and the Middle East and eventually landed in Kathmandu. I carried a little notebook, writing poetry. I had a beard and ponytail and wore dark hippie sunglasses. I was feeling my way through the semidarkness toward the light that I sort of intuited but couldn't really see. I began to get a feeling "it" was "out there"—at least for me. I traveled around Asia for a while and I still didn't know what I was doing, but over the months the need to know was becoming less and less, while an inner certainty was growing.

In Allahabad, I met Neem Karoli Baba (Ram Dass' guru) through John and Mirabai Bush. He became my guru and gave me my name, Surya Das, after a blind Indian devotional poet in the middle ages. It means "servant of the sun" or "disciple of the light." I began going to Goenka's ten-day *vipassana* meditation courses. Fortunately, the Bushes hadn't told me how strict and demanding it was before we went there. It wasn't like the Zen meditations, which were fairly short sittings, some walking meditation, and a little talking. At Goenka-ji's retreat, it was daily twelve hours of meditation in silence, one hour of sitting at a time, no food after noon, noble silence, and other monastic strictures. But I never felt so peaceful in my life and I've been meditating ever since. It changed my life. It's much easier to practice in an *ashram* or meditation center than in the outside world, so he urged us to take a vow to meditate every day. Young people who are still my companions on the path, like Sharon Salzberg, Daniel Goleman, Joseph Goldstein, Jack Engler, Christopher Titmus, and Krishna Das, were also there.

I went on to Nepal to meet Tibetan *lamas* and I began reading *The Tibetan Book of the Dead*. In Nepal I met Lama Thubten Yeshe and stayed at his Kopan monastery on a hilltop outside Kathmandu. I still go there every few years. I made some great Dharma friends, had a lot of spiritual experiences and even magical dreams and visions. Lama Yeshe became my first real teacher. He urged us to become monks and to learn Tibetan. It seemed a little much to become an ordained, celibate, shave-pate monk for life at that time. Lama Yeshe suggested, "Why don't you do a retreat?" so I said, "Why not?" For several years after that, on and off, I sat in a little clay, thatched hut and he came to visit me every day. I was doing preliminary Tibetan practices like chanting *mantras*, prayers, and bowing as well as sitting vipassana.

One day, Lama Yeshe suggested, "Why don't you meet the Dalai Lama?" He gave me a letter of introduction. It was an eighteen-hour train ride across northern India. The train uncoupled while I was blissfully asleep in the luggage rack above the third class wooden seats. My car was re-coupled onto another train and ended up going to a different place. So as I say, even though I thought I knew where I was going, I didn't know where I was going. My car ended up in Hardwar, near Rishikesh, at the top of the Ganges. There must be a reason. I ended up living at Swami Sivananda's ashram by the Ganges in Rishikesh for a few weeks doing yoga and chanting.

I had my twenty-first birthday in Nepal in my thatched hut under the stars. I could have been lonely but I wasn't. I was happy. This was a big turning point for me. I was alone but not lonely. I always had a little bit of good *karma,* being blessed and protected. Other people I knew who came to Asia fell off cliffs and died, were in bus accidents, plane hijackings and crashes, had passport problems, got mugged, raped on the road in those poor countries... but nothing like that ever happened to me. Eventually I remembered His Holiness the Dalai Lama, left the ashram and found my way to Dharamsala.

I still remember the day that I had that appointment with the Dalai Lama, in late June of '72. As I was walking on a dirt path to go there, my *mala* broke. The beads fell in the mud and I was trying to pick them up one by one. Time was running out. I was thinking, "Oh, I really can't be late for the Dalai Lama and I know there's other people going and I have my appointment hour and I have to get there. But how can I go in"—it's just like a young seeker—"*how can I go see the Dalai Lama without my mala beads?!* I've been wearing my mala beads for *a whole year* and it shows that I'm a Serious Buddhist Practitioner. I can't go without *my mala beads!*" But the beads were stuck in the mud. The Dalai Lama was waiting. I picked up a few beads, put them in my pocket and went to see the Dalai Lama. There's a teaching in that, about what's important and what isn't. Looks and accoutrements are definitely not important.

I had a wonderful interview with His Holiness. I was used to seeing lamas and saints, bowing at their feet, and presenting an offering. The Dalai Lama didn't allow that. He stood up from his couch, met me at the door, shook my hand, and led me over to sit next to him on his couch. That was pretty impressive. The forty-five-minute private audience proceeded from there. When people ask me, I always say that he's the humblest person I ever met. That was my first impression and it hasn't changed. He was very, very interested in what I was doing. He said, "Thank you so much for meditating and doing what you're doing. I have a lot of political work, concerns about my exiled Tibetan people, but I hope when I retire I'll have time to study and practice Buddhism." It was powerful, inspiring, touching. After that I resolved to go back to my lamas and really practice.

I had plenty of questions and doubts about which rules, vows, precepts, and worldviews—like beliefs in reincarnation, other worlds, invisible beings, the lower realms—made sense and were worth adopting. The Dalai Lama encouraged me to ask these questions and explore Buddhism. He said that Buddhism would reveal itself. That encouraged me to really use my questioning, analytical intellect to understand and go deeper into Buddhism, to find out the truth, to not just take on a set of beliefs, to not swallow it whole.

All this time while I was in Asia, my parents were going crazy, missing me, feeling concerned, not understanding what I could be doing for so long instead of graduate studies and a career and family life. But, as my Jewish mother says, "After a few decades, you can get used to anything." My aunt would say, "Jeffrey, for every year you spent in India, your mother got ten years worth of gray hair." They wanted me to become a doctor, have 2.2 children and a nice house in the suburbs, and if I wanted to go to India for two weeks on vacation, that'd be nice . . . but why not Israel? It was hard for them. But when I was in Japan in '75, they actually came and visited, and they saw how I was treated. I had a lot of respect as a college English teacher, poet, and Buddhist scholar. They're Jewish, but they think I'm more religious than anyone in the family and that means something good to them. They brag to people about their son the author, and more amusingly, "My son, the lama."

When you are on the path, as you grow up and separate from your family you have to follow your own star if you want to find your true vocation. It is not possible to just stay in the past and inherit or imitate the business of your parents. That can be painful on both sides. The truth is that parents want their children to be safe and happy, bottom line. It is up to oneself to pursue that.

It is a challenge today to bring the Dharma into daily life, integrating spiritual practice with work and family and our speedy, post-modern and tech society. I respect anyone that can practice while they go to school or hold down a job. I had the fortune to cultivate my practice in monasteries and ashrams, keeping a very simple life. I learned to do without, like not having new clothes, credit cards, technological tools and gadgetry, family, or vacations. It took some sacrifice, but it was not overly hard. In those days, I didn't live in a way that I had to make a living. I was graciously received by my Tibetan master's family and in monasteries and ashrams, however poor they may have been themselves. By being single and homeless I've learned how much one can do without and how simple life can be, to the extent we can learn to let go and learn to be authentically ourselves. Everything we need we can find within.

There was an advantage to being young. I didn't have anything else to do. I didn't have to make a living because I didn't need much. I didn't have rent, mortgage, or car payments, I had no health insurance, didn't have to support dependents. When you're young, you have your health, energy, and time. Time is the most precious commodity you have; time is life. It's hard to get it back once you lose it. It's hard to keep once you form the habit of squandering it. Killing time is like deadening ourselves and wasting our precious, marvelous life.

I was like a spiritual slut in those halcyon days. I did it—spiritually, I mean—with all the great gurus of India. It was good in the beginning, and even in the middle, of my spiritual path to do a little shopping around, compare, try things on, return it if it didn't fit. At a certain point, commitment can bring a lot of rewards, just as in relationship. You don't want to marry the first person you fall in love with or even have sex with. At a certain point, though, it could become worth making a deeper commitment. Without commitment, it is difficult to sink roots in deep enough to get the nutrients and to really grow. Without deep roots, it is difficult to grow tall.

It is useful and sane to window shop. It is okay to ask questions, sniff around, join and leave. Don't just sign your life away, don't join a cult you can't get out of. Just join this center, sign up for that newsletter, go to a retreat or ashram or Sufi dancing or synagogue or church. If it doesn't work for you, it's not the only way. Not all of us are joiners, some of us have to follow our own path. These days, we live in a melting-pot society and have melting-pot karma, so we have melting-pot Dharma. As long as we're aware of it, we can avoid the pitfalls of superficiality and mere dilettantism. We don't want to quit whenever the going gets tough; then you never really get there. It can be uncomfortable, it will bring up your fears. That's where teachers and teachings, friends and *sangha* can come in. They can guide us so that we don't have to figure it all out ourselves. Gradually, we go more into the practicing and the finding and less into the hungrily seeking.

Buddhism set me on the path to inner peace. I had taken lots of drugs, but I didn't know I could be so serene through meditation. From the first Goenka retreat, I found meditation to be noninvasive, non-illegal, and healthy. It was natural rather than something corrupting. Wow, what else would I want to do with my life? Meditation was a breakthrough to a way of being that I couldn't imagine by reading Eastern philosophy, that I couldn't get access to through reading and thinking. I wanted to be like the white-haired Tibetan masters. That possibility was immediate, not far away. Meditation enhances everything, rather than it being a chore or something to get out of the way. It gave me a whole different way of being—serenity, love, knowing life as wisdom and oneness rather than struggle and resistance. This has been irresistible.

How I Became a Buddhist Nun

Venerable Yifa

The story of how I first came to Buddhism may be somewhat surprising. There was no sudden light from the heavens, no hidden celestial voice; there wasn't even a deep-seated sense of vocation drawing me away from secular society. In fact, it could be said that it was not even a "spiritual" calling at all—at least not in the most widely understood sense of the word.

As early as my middle-school years, I can remember being especially curious as to the purpose of life, pondering this question with great intensity and seeking its answers in all that I saw around me. Most adults, I had noticed, felt it important to throw themselves into their work so they could be assured of making a living. And yet it seemed to me that most of these same people ended up living only to work. Though I appreciated the need for work, there was still something about this process that struck me as being rather pointless.

And yet, I grew to be an ambitious youth when it came to thoughts of a career. I entertained hopes of becoming a politician

Venerable Yifa, 43, a Taiwanese Buddhist nun in the Fo Guang Shan, teaches in the U.S. and is the author of Safeguarding the Heart: A Buddhist Response to Suffering and September 11.

in my home country of Taiwan, and consequently I spent the first year of higher education studying political science, an interest that soon translated into a study of law. It didn't take me long to realize what it was in these disciplines that really interested me. More than learning about political government and law in and of themselves, I wished to discover insight into those laws that govern the very way in which the world operates at large. In short, I saw in the study of law—whether civil, social, or natural—a means for exploring the nature of Truth. It was this philosophical aspect of my academic pursuits that seemed most rewarding to that inquisitive middle-school girl still within me.

Then came a turning point in my life. But, this was not, as one might expect, the point at which I dropped my legal studies to pursue a higher calling. On the contrary, it can be said that this turning point was the moment at which I fully realized *why* I was studying law, and to what end I would now harness my interest in that discipline.

In 1979, a friend invited me to go on a two-week retreat to a Buddhist monastery. The suggested trip seemed a pleasant way of spending part of a summer and so I acquiesced, expecting an outing where I'd meet people and enjoy a different experience. In my lifelong search for answers to the great philosophical questions, I had never considered looking for insight in any church or temple. After all, in my experience, such places were little more than bastions of superstition, the primary value of which was the providing of comfort to the elderly and emotional palliatives to those who need help coping with life. As I would soon discover, however, I was wrong.

At the monastic retreat of the Fo Guang Shan Buddhist Temple, I first learned the power of meditation and chanting. Completely ignorant of Buddhism as I was, I attended numerous lectures on the Dharma. Before long, it began to dawn on me that the essence of Buddhism is not concerned with superstition but with wisdom, with the search for the same universal laws that had interested me in my youth and in my academic career. As such, Buddhism was every bit as applicable and useful to my life as it was to my grandmother's.

I quickly came to regret the fact that I had not pursued this path long before, and inwardly vowed henceforth to support Buddhism as much as possible throughout my otherwise secular life. As the retreat continued, I even began to understand why so many elderly Taiwanese women become nuns in their autumn years, as many of them must have found late in life the need for the same sort of wisdom I was now seeking.

But once I caught myself thinking this way, a new thought occurred to me as well. Why should I avoid further study if I felt this way now, if I already saw the possibility of something profoundly rewarding in a personal life in Buddhism? Was not any postponement or circumscription of a more serious devotion to the ways of the Dharma on my part little more than the reinforcement of the very phenomenon that had kept me from Buddhism in the first place? After all, I had just had the revelation that Buddhism was not a religion strictly for the elderly or the superstitious, but a search for universal laws, and as such it applied not to a select segment of society, but to the entire universe. Surely, people of every age and station would find this religion useful—and it was with an eye to making myself useful that I decided upon my next logical step in life.

I resolved that the most efficient way to seek and spread truth and justice was for me to renounce the things that had formerly driven me—the desire for fame and power in a career—and to become a nun myself in the Buddhist tradition. At last, here was a path by which I could truly study the law in its greatest sense, a path that for me grew directly out of my earlier, secular pursuits.

In fact, my former interests now made the choice to become a nun all the more fitting and worthwhile. As a young person studying at a respected Taiwanese university, I might be a great asset to the Buddhist religion in my country, and could thereby further its goals throughout the nation and the world.

However, my parents had other ideas. Hitherto pleased with the general progress of my academic career, they saw my joining a Buddhist temple as the abandonment of everything that had been of benefit to my life. When I joined the Buddhist order at the age of twenty, I was still a student in law school. My renunciation was beyond my parents' comprehension, and they opposed my decision. They took great pains to dissuade me, and even took physical steps to block my tonsure, essentially trying to keep me under virtual house arrest for two months in hopes of breaking down my resolve. As my choice to become a monastic seemed utterly irrational to them, my parents came to believe that I must somehow be possessed of a cursed spirit of some sort, and they tried numerous methods of "curing" me.

I recall that my father, whose thinking is strongly influenced by Confucian philosophy, challenged me by asking a question: if I was going to be a nun living in a monastery, how I was going to repay my debt of gratitude to family, school, and society, all of which had raised me and had provided for my education? I replied that by joining the order without a future family of my own, I could devote myself completely to society. My father did not say a word in response.

Growing up in Taiwan, I thought Buddhism was something that was practiced in a temple or a monastery and bore no relevance to daily life with its ambitions, stresses, and hectic pace. Indeed, I thought people who practiced Buddhism wanted to escape from society and life and found the temple was a shelter. Thus, I was shocked and amazed when I saw how young the monks and nuns at the Fo Guang Shan Temple were. Not only were they young—in their twenties and thirties—but they seemed joyous and energetic as well.

After my ordination, which was a moment of great pride for me, I settled fully into life in the community. Many people find living with a group of others all day long to be difficult, but for me it was remarkably easy. All of the novices had to go through a kind of basic training—such as learning to cook and clean—so that we could share the work. However, because the life was simple, these tasks were not too arduous and we could pursue our other interests as well.

I enjoy being a nun. When I first entered the monastic life, some people told me that in order to flourish within the monastery I would need to have been a monk or nun in a previous life. At the time I was not convinced, but now I think there might be something to their idea—if only because I have never felt uncomfortable or anxious within the setting.

As a nun, I do not feel any different from when I was a layperson. Living the simple life has helped me concentrate more easily on my academic pursuits, such as finishing college, law school, and completing a Ph.D. And it has also enabled me to focus effectively on my spiritual pursuits, such as studying the *sutras,* meditating, and lecturing on Buddhist knowledge.

After several years in Taiwan, during which I finished my law degree, the head of my order and I agreed that I should go to the United States to propagate the Dharma of Humanistic Buddhism, a variety of Buddhism which teaches that one can live fully in this human world and practice Buddhism at the same time. I went first to Hawaii and then Connecticut and Yale. This was both a spiritual and secular mission. I felt that the United States was a good place to propagate the Dharma, and I wanted to enhance my knowledge of the Chinese Buddhist tradition by using the analytical methods of critical inquiry practiced in the West. I ended up taking a Ph.D. in religious studies at Yale University.

Yale was an enormous challenge for me. First of all, I had to immerse myself in the English language, which was not an easy task. Secondly, I was, as you can imagine, not only the only Buddhist nun on campus, but (it seemed) in all of New Haven. It was difficult at times for me to live in a college dormitory, because many of the students were unsure of how to approach me and kept their distance. When I received my doctoral degree from Yale, my parents, as well as my eldest brother and sister, flew to the East Coast to attend my graduation. On this occasion, my father told me that he was very proud of me. Due to my accomplishment, my parents respectively received the "Father and Mother of the Year" award in my hometown. I had made good on my promise to my parents.

Then at Hsi Lai University, a new institute founded by Fo Guang Shan in Los Angeles, I became the Provost in developing programs for this. I followed that up by being a visiting scholar at the University of California at Berkeley and Harvard University. I now travel the world, teaching the ideas of Humanistic Buddhism.

I have never wanted to be treated in a different manner because I am a nun, and feel that the Dharma is best spread when it is fully integrated into the society around it. The idea of the lotus—which grows in the muddy pond and yet whose beautiful flower emerges above the surface of the water—was a powerful image for me in those days as I negotiated the tricky balancing act of being a monastic in a non-monastic setting. That image enabled me to remain true to my calling; many monks and nuns, after they enter the secular world, are attracted by it and drawn into intimate relationships and disrobe. I, on the other hand, wanted to maintain my monastic status and integrate myself into society. The spiritual practices that have been part of my daily life as a nun have allowed me to discipline my mind and concentrate my attention to enhance the quality of my life on a day-to-day basis, so that I neither need to be in a monastic setting nor disrobe.

Many young people today are uncertain as to how to live their lives. They feel restless and unhappy at the direction that they see the world going in. In my experience, monasticism is not a flight *from* the world, but an engagement with the deepest directions *of* the world. Through my monastic training—in combination with the critical tools and rich life experiences that I have had in the West—I feel that I am better able to look at what is wrong with the world and provide some solutions for how to make it better.

Stories of a Young Zen Monk

Thich Nhat Hanh

Let me tell you about the temple where I lived as a novice monk in Vietnam. My temple followed the Zen tradition. Therefore, every one of us from the highest monk to the newest member equally followed the principle of "no work, no food." Those who joined the temple had to pass a period of taking care of the cows for at least three months. Tending the cattle was a relatively easy task compared to polishing rice. This was a manual process that required a team effort of four or five people, each pounding grains of rice in a large mortar with big pestles to whiten the grain. As far as my young monk friend Brother Man (*Man* is a Vietnamese name) and I were concerned, these pestles were too heavy. Yet it had to be lifted and pounded in rhythm and at the right time. When the pestle wasn't well aimed, the rice would jump everywhere. After fifty or sixty hits with the pestle, our entire bodies would be exhausted and we'd be soaked in sweat. It was clearly the worst job. Then there were other kinds of work that everyone had to do. For example, there was hulling rice and digging earth to grow the different types of potatoes.

Thich Nhat Hanh, 76, is a Zen master, poet, and peace and human rights activist. He founded the Order of Interbeing.

We all worked, but we didn't work all day. There was time for us to study the *sutras,* practice writing, listen to the teachings given by our teacher, chant, and meditate. Most important was meditation. My teacher taught that meditation was the door to understanding, and that it was the career of monks and nuns. Of course you did not practice sitting meditation all day when you entered the temple. For months and sometimes years you had to take care of the cows, collect dry twigs and leaves, carry water, pound rice, and collect wood for the fire. Every time my mother came to visit from our village, which was far away, she would regard these things as being the challenges of the first stage of practice. At first my mother was concerned for my health, but as I grew healthier, she stopped worrying about me. As for me, I knew that these were not challenges—they were themselves the practice. If you enter this life, you will see for yourself.

My friend Brother Man saw it in the same way as I did, and later in life the two of us would look back on our novice years with deep affection, joy, and gratitude. But I remember very clearly how lost I felt when I first came to the monastery; it was so different from the ordinary world. The atmosphere was silent and at the same time energetic, solemn but also gentle. On first entering a monastery, a person sees everyone else there as leisurely, upright, gentle, and joyful in a solemn manner. It makes the person feel even more clumsy. If a *dieu* (the Vietnamese word for "novice") were to bang a door shut just once, for example, he would be reprimanded right away. We learned and practiced mindful manners by observing and listening to our elders. We learned by watching the way the brother who cared for the altar opened and closed the door with gentle, slow movements when he went out of his room, as though he were afraid of causing unnecessary noise in the monastery. We examined our actions, language, and thoughts while we were walking, standing, sitting, or lying down. We ourselves became aware of our every move—body, speech, and mind.

————————

At the time that I asked permission to enter the temple as a novice, there were just four of us aspirants in a temple of thirty. We all studied and worked together. In our first year we studied the daily liturgy and precepts of novices. In our second year we studied the commentaries on the precepts and well-known sutras. By the third year, of the four of us, Brother Man and I had excelled in our studies and we had great hopes of being the first to have novice ordination. That moment finally came. One evening as I was carrying wood back to the temple, I was given the good news by a brother. My teacher, the elder of the community, would officially transmit to me novice ordination and I would be sent to the Institute of Buddhist Studies of Bao Quoc.

In my joy, there was all the elation of youth. Suddenly I felt more mature and important. My ordination was scheduled for four o'clock the next morning. That night after the *sangha*'s Pure Land chanting practice, I saw my teacher sitting in his room on a cushion beside the light of a flickering candle; there was a stack of old scriptures piled high on a table next to him. He was carefully mending a tear in an old brown robe. Despite his old age, he still had clear vision and a straight posture. Brother Man and I stopped at the entrance and watched. As he slowly pulled the needle through the cloth, my teacher looked like a *bodhisattva* in deep meditation.

After a moment we entered the room and my teacher looked up. Seeing us, he nodded and then lowered his head to continue sewing a half-sewn stitch. Brother Man spoke: "Respected teacher, please go and rest, it is already very late." My teacher did not look up. "Let me finish sewing this robe so that Quan can wear it tomorrow morning." Then I understood why my teacher had been sorting through his pile of old robes all afternoon; he was looking for the least worn robe to fix and make presentable for me. Tomorrow for the first time I would wear a brown robe. During the past three years we were only allowed to wear the gray robe. Once ordained as a novice, I would be allowed to put on the precious robe that the sutras call the robe of liberation, the uniform of freedom.

In a wavering voice I said, "Respected teacher, let us ask Auntie Tu to finish the sewing." "No, I want to sew it for you with my own hands," he replied, softly. There was silence. With our arms folded in an obedient manner we stood to one side not daring to say another word.

A little later my teacher, without raising his eyes from the needle, spoke, "Have you heard the story in the sutras about a great disciple during the time of the Buddha who attained enlightenment just from sewing robes? Let me tell it to you," he continued. "This disciple often found joy and peace in mending torn robes; he mended his own and also those of his Dharma brothers. Each time he passed the needle through the fabric, he gave rise to a wholesome goodness that had the power to liberate. One day, when the needle was passing through the fabric, he understood thoroughly a deep and most wonderful teaching, and in six consecutive stitches he attained the six miraculous powers." I turned my head and looked at my teacher with deep affection and respect. My teacher might not have attained the six miraculous powers, but he had reached a profound stage that who knew how long it would take us to achieve.

At last the robe was mended. My teacher signaled for me to come closer. My teacher handed me the robe. I received it knowing it was a tremendous encouragement and given with a tender love. My teacher's voice at that moment was probably the gentlest and sweetest I had ever heard: "I mended this myself so that tomorrow you will have it to wear, my child." He asked me to try it on. The robe was a little too large for me, but that did not stop me from feeling so happy that I was moved to tears. I was touched. Living the path of practice, I received the most sacred kind of love—a pure love that was gentle and spacious, which nourished and made fragrant my aspiration throughout my many years of training and practice.

One day, the abbot and *bhikshus* (the Sanskrit word for a Buddhist monk) from the temple left early in the morning to attend an assembly. The temple was almost empty; only Brother Man and I were left. I was writing up my studies when Brother Man came to tell me that there was a guest.

"There's a young man asking to see the abbot," he said. "I don't know whether to ask him to stay or not."

I put down my pen and replied, "You can ask him to stay, Brother. Invite him into the guest house. I'll be there in a few moments."

I put on my robe and went to greet him. The young man was looking at a painting of the bodhisattva Avalokiteshvara. He looked contemplative. Hearing me enter, he turned around and stood up. I invited him to sit and poured him some tea. I asked him if there was anything urgent that needed to be passed on to my teacher. He quickly replied that there was nothing urgent. Then he sat still, quietly observing all the things on display in the guest house. I also sat silently, without asking him further questions.

Suddenly he asked, "How long have you been a monk, Brother?"

"I've been a monk for almost three years," I said, looking at him.

"How old were you when you came?"

"Nineteen."

"So this year you are twenty-two years old. I just turned twenty-three," he said. "I'm a little older than you." His voice suddenly became soft and intimate. "You must regard me as your brother," he said, "and not be angry if I ask too many personal questions."

I laughed. "I wouldn't think of it. Please go ahead and ask."

He was quiet for a moment and then he asked, "Why did you become a monk?"

I raised my eyes, looked at him, and felt slightly uncomfortable. But quickly I came back to myself and answered directly, "Because I like Buddhism and its teaching of mindful living. I was born in a Buddhist family and had the chance to read about Buddhism in books and magazines. I found myself naturally drawn to the ideal of liberation in Buddhism and to this lifestyle, especially when I learned it could help us understand reality as it is."

As he listened attentively, I noticed there was some sadness he was trying to hide. Afraid that I would see his sadness, he took a deep breath. Finally, he said quietly, "I have a friend who wants to become a monk, but my friend doesn't know if there are any requirements."

"How old is your friend?" I asked.

"Around the same age as you and me."

"Is your friend still a student?"

"Yes, he has completed the first half of the baccalaureate degree. So, Brother, do you know what it takes for my friend to become a monk? What does he need in order to be ordained?"

"About the requirements..." I said, hesitating, "there really aren't that many." Then unexpectedly, I asked, "Has your friend been disappointed in love or something?" My question was so unexpected it embarrassed him. He looked completely bewildered. I felt compassion for him.

"If your friend is disappointed in love," I continued, "he wouldn't be encouraged to ordain."

"Why is that, Brother?"

"Because he would not be able to endure the life of a monk," I replied.

"Why not?" he asked.

"Because he lacks a strong will. He wants to be a monk now because he has been disappointed in love. That is what many people do—having failed in an endeavor, they become weary of life and want to escape it altogether. If a person is disappointed and weary of life, it means a strong will is lacking. And if there is no strong will, how is it possible to live the life of someone who needs to practice perseverance and perhaps endure some hardship?"

"My friend will not be afraid of a life of hardship," he replied.

"It is not physical hardship I'm talking about, it's a strong commitment to withstand trials and be able to make an effort to reach the goal of a spiritual path. If it is because of a disappointment in love that your friend turns to the spiritual path, sooner or later he'll give that up too."

"Please, Brother, say more."

"First of all, your friend would be entering the monastery with a heavy heart and a great sadness. That in itself is not right. While others have entered the monastic life with clarity and a sincere aspiration to take the vows, your friend instead enters the monastery with the intention of escaping and turning away from the world. The practice community is not a refuge for souls saddened by disappointment."

"But doesn't Buddhism help those who are suffering?" he asked.

"That is true. But there are many ways of helping. Those who do not share the concerns of the Sangha cannot be a part of the Sangha."

"Please tell me what these concerns are."

"As I've said, the purpose is to gain liberation and awakening for oneself and others. In this case, your friend does not have that intention. He only wants to escape life. But the Dharma came into being to live life. To practice as monks is to train ourselves in mindfulness and awakening, to first free ourselves from suffering and then to help others do the same."

"Who knows," he said, "later on my friend might be able to share this aspiration and achieve its goal."

"That's something we can't foretell. But if he entered the monastic life now, he would suffer more than if he remained in the world. We feel free, at peace, and happy, living in a peaceful environment such as this; but your friend, on the other hand, would suffer miserably precisely because of this very peace and quiet. The more solitary the place he lives, the more he'll have to confront his sadness and despair, and the more he will suffer. We enjoy hearing the sound of the bell, and it makes us feel more peaceful and concentrated each time we hear it—whereas for your friend, the sound of the bell would make him feel mournful because his soul is wounded and not as whole as those around him."

It was lunch and Brother Man had just finished the offering to the Buddha. Our young guest expressed regret that we would have to stop our conversation, so I warmly invited him to stay for lunch. His eyes brightened. There were just the three of us at lunch. Brother Man had thoughtfully asked Auntie Tu earlier on to prepare an extra dish of young bamboo shoots and include it in our meal.

After lunch, Vinh (it was at lunchtime that we finally learned our guest's name) wanted to continue our talk. The three of us walked out to the hills and sat down under a row of pine trees. I introduced Brother Man to Vinh. Together we talked with Vinh as though we had known him for a long time.

He asked us, "Have you read *An Afternoon Went By* by Nhat Linh?"

"Yes, I have," I said. "Your mentioning this book must mean you have understood what I told you this morning. The nun in Nhat Linh's book became a nun because she had been disappointed in love. Living in a peaceful environment, hearing the bells, she never felt a bit at ease. It was the opposite for her—she suffered even more, she became more broken. Therefore, when she left the monastery with a visitor, it wasn't surprising. Luckily she was just a character in a novel. We do not want people like this in the monastery."

Unintentionally, my words made Vinh blush. He turned away and pretended to look in the direction of the temple tower. But Brother Man was quick to see his embarrassment and tried to lighten things up. "It might be evening before the elder brothers return," he said.

Vinh suddenly turned back toward us and said, "Then my friend shouldn't ordain?"

"Right, he really shouldn't," I replied. "He should try to free himself from the shell of his clouded mind that he's been caught in. Life is beautiful but your friend does not see it. Look at us—we enjoy our life as monks, we have our aspirations and a spiritual path. We want to live our ideal. There are only two things we try to avoid: we want to free ourselves from craving and delusion. Your friend should free himself from his broken heart, and the sooner the better. That will help the deepest and most wholesome aspirations in him to manifest."

Brother Man smiled and asked Vinh, "To want to be a monk just because someone betrayed you, do you think that is a good motivation?"

Vinh replied, softly, "Shouldn't we at least feel some compassion for him?"

"Yes, of course, we should feel compassion for him."

"If my friend would no longer want to ordain but only wanted to learn about the monastic life, is it still a bad idea, Brother Man?"

"That, you'll need to ask Brother Quan."

"Of course it's not bad. Quite the opposite, we would sympathize with him. And if he would like to come to the monastery from time to time to learn more about the Dharma and to participate in the practice, we would be delighted," I replied.

Vinh laughed, joyfully. "Then for sure I'll bring my friend along. He'll probably love you brothers."

Two days later Vinh returned, but he came alone. It turned out that his friend and himself were the same person. He looked fresher and younger than he had looked on the previous visit. "Thanks, Brother," he said, "for liberating me from a dark situation. Your words as well as your way of being relieved my sorrow and the weariness I felt. When I returned home that day, I thought a lot about what you had said. I saw that I was almost drowning in my darkness. My encounter with you brought about much healing. I feel lighter now. I can study and I can smile again. I have rediscovered the joy of living."

"But I still doubt that you have completely healed."

"Yes, but I can say I am on the way to total recovery. You do not know how much I was suffering in the past two months."

"But now you have benefited from a few drops of the compassionate nectar of the Dharma. I hope you have a chance to study and practice the Dharma and discover more about the beauty and depth of this path of compassion."

"I would like to learn more about Buddhism. For a long time, I had many wrong views—I thought Buddhism was a place for the sorrowful and weary soul. I would like to go deeper."

Who would have guessed that this young man needed only one drop of the Dharma's nectar of compassion to be reborn into a joyful life?

Daniel Marty, a young Frenchman, and I were brought together by fate near my beloved temple Bao Quoc in 1947 (I was about twenty-one, then). The road from my school to my home temple was very treacherous. The French army occupied all of the Nam Giao region and had set up a military base there. People living high in the hills had set up small fortresses for protection. There were times when gunshots were exchanged between French and Vietnamese soldiers. There were nights when the villagers shut themselves in their homes, bracing against the barrage of gunfire. And in the morning when they awoke, they found corpses near Nam Giao from the battle of the previous night, with slogans written in whitewash mixed with blood on the road. It was during these tumultuous times that Daniel and I met. I was a Vietnamese student monk and he was a young French army soldier.

One morning, I was walking the road back to my temple. It was quite early; the dew was still on the tips of the grass. Inside my cloth bag I carried my robe and a few sutras. In my hand I held a cone-shaped straw hat. I felt light and joyful at the thought of visiting my temple and seeing my teacher and Brother Man, and the ancient, venerated temple. I had just crossed a hill when a voice called out. On the hill above the road, I saw a French soldier waving. Thinking he was making fun of me because I was a monk, I turned my back to him and continued down the road. But suddenly I had the feeling that this was no joking matter. Behind me I heard the clomping of soldier's boots as someone ran towards me. Perhaps he wanted to search me; the cloth bag I was carrying may have looked suspicious to him. I stopped walking and waited. A young soldier with a handsome and intelligent face approached me.

"Where are you going?" he asked. Hearing his poor pronunciation I surmised that he probably knew only a few words in Vietnamese.

I laughed and asked him in French, "If I reply in Vietnamese, would you understand?"

Seeing that I could speak French, his face beamed. He let me know that he had no intention of searching me, and that he only wanted to ask me something. I asked what that was, and he replied, "I want to know which temple you're from."

"I'm from Bao Quoc Temple," I replied.

"Bao Quoc Temple? Is that the big temple on the hill near the train station?"

"That's the one," I said.

He pointed up to a water pump house on the side of the hill and said, "If you're not too busy, please come up there with me so we can talk for a little while." We sat down near the pump house and he told me about the visit he and five other soldiers had made ten days earlier to Bao Quoc Temple. They went to the temple at ten o'clock at night in search of Vietnamese resistors who were reportedly gathering at the temple.

"We were determined to find them. We carried guns. The orders were to arrest and even kill if necessary. But when we entered the temple we were utterly shocked."

"Because there were so many Viet Minh?"

"No! No!" he exclaimed, "We wouldn't have been shocked if we had seen Viet Minh. We would have attacked no matter how many there were."

It sounded very strange. "So what shocked you?"

"What happened this time was so unexpected. Wherever we did searches in the past, people would run away or be thrown into a state of panic."

"It's because the people have been terrorized so many times that they run away in fear," I said.

"I myself don't make a habit of terrorizing or threatening

people," he replied. "Perhaps it was because they have been harmed by those who came before us that they are so frightened.

"When we entered the temple," he continued, "it was like entering a deserted place. The oil lamps were turned very low. It was completely silent. We purposely stomped our feet loudly on the gravel, but there was no other sound. I had the feeling there were many people in the temple, but it was completely quiet apart from the ticking of a clock that was hanging nearby. The shouting of a comrade made me uneasy. No one made a reply. I pointed my flashlight into the empty room, and before our eyes appeared a solemn scene of fifty or sixty monks sitting still and silently in meditation."

"It was because you came during our sitting period," I said, nodding my head.

"Yes, it was like we ran into a strange and invisible force," he said. "It scared us so much that we turned and left the temple. The monks just ignored us! They didn't raise a voice in reply and they didn't show any signs of panic or fear."

"They weren't ignoring you, they were practicing concentrating on their breath, that was all."

"We ourselves were attracted to their calmness—it was worthy of our respect. We stood silently in the temple's courtyard at the foot of a large tree and waited for perhaps a half an hour. There were a series of bells that sounded, and then the temple returned to normal activity. A monk lit a torch and came to invite us inside, but we simply told him why we were there and then asked to leave. From that day on I began to change my ideas about the Vietnamese people.

"There are many young men about our age among us," he began. "We are homesick; we miss our families and country a lot. We have been sent here to kill the Viet Minh, but we don't know if we will kill them or we will be killed by them and never return home to our families. Seeing the people here work so hard to rebuild their shattered lives reminds me of the shattered lives of my relatives in France. The peaceful and serene life of those Vietnamese monks makes me think about the lives of all human beings on this Earth. And I wonder why we have come here. What is this hatred between the Viet Minh and us that we have come all this way to fight them?"

Deeply moved, I took the hand of the young soldier. I told him a story of an old friend of mine who had enlisted to fight the French, and who had been successful in winning many battles. One day my friend came to the temple and burst into tears as he embraced me. He told me that during an attack on a fortress, while he was concealed behind some rocks, he saw two young French soldiers sitting and talking. "When I saw the bright, handsome, and innocent faces of those young boys," he said, "I couldn't bear to open fire, dear Brother. People can label me weak and soft, they can say that if all the Vietnamese fighters were like me, it wouldn't be long before our whole country was overtaken. But, for a moment I had loved the enemy like my own mother loves me! I knew that the deaths of these two youngsters would make their mothers in France suffer, just as my mother had grieved for the death of my younger brother."

"So you see," I said, "the young Vietnamese soldier's heart was filled with the love of humanity."

The young French soldier was lost in thought for a moment.

Perhaps like me, he had realized the absurdity of the killing, the calamity of war, and that young men were dying in an unjust and heartbreaking way.

The sun had already risen high in the sky and it was time to go. Before going he told me that his name was Daniel Marty and he was twenty-one years old. He had just finished high school before he came to Vietnam. He showed me photographs of his mother and a younger brother and sister. We parted with a feeling of understanding between us and he promised to visit me at the temple on Sundays.

From then on our friendship continued to deepen. I spoke to him about Buddhism and he let me borrow books on Buddhism written by Rhys-Davies, Neel, and La Vallee Poussin. He had an affinity towards Buddhism and wanted to live the way of a Buddhist. I took him to the Buddha Hall for prostration practice and I gave him the Dharma name Thanh Luong. He was very happy when I explained the meaning of the name, "Pure and Refreshing Peaceful Life." Whenever he saw me he joined his palms in greeting just like any Buddhist.

One day, Brother Man suggested that we invite our friend to a vegetarian meal at the temple. Thanh Luong accepted the invitation happily. Our Dharma friend highly praised the delicious black olives and the flavorful dishes we served him. He found the fragrant mushroom rice soup Brother Man had prepared so delicious that he couldn't believe it was vegetarian. I had to explain to him in detail how it was made before he would believe that it was true.

There were days when, sitting beside the temple tower, we would delve into conversations on spirituality and literature. When I praised French literature, Thanh Luong's eyes lit up with pride of his nation's culture. I outlined a short history of Vietnamese literature for him from its foundation in ancient times. Our friendship was becoming very deep. Then one day when he came to visit, he announced that his unit would be moving to another area and it was likely that he would be able to return to France. Our farewell was sad and compassionate. "I'll never forget your gentle face, Brother," he said. "Buddhism has made your spirit calm and gentle, pure and compassionate. I don't know if I will ever be able to see you again."

I walked him to the gate under the arch of the three portals of Bao Quoc Temple and looked him in the eye as I spoke. "No matter where you are, if you keep the Dharma in mind then I will always be beside you. The Dharma has brought us together to understand and like one another. I am certain your heart will always be bright and wholesome because there is a Buddha in you. As children of the Buddha, we will never be parted."

"I will write you, Brother."

"And I will be very happy to receive your letter."

A month later I received a letter from him with news that he would return to France, then go to Algeria. He promised to write to me from there.

I have not heard from him since then. Who knows where Thanh Luong, that child of the Buddha, is now. Is he safe? But I have faith that no matter what situation he is in, he is at peace. The lives of all living beings filled his own heart, and like my Vietnamese friend, he too saw the meaninglessness and destructiveness of war.

Journey to Mindfulness

BHANTE HENEPOLA GUNARATANA

I've read a few life stories of spiritual men and women, and it always seems like miraculous, wondrous things happen to the main character. Reading these amazing stories, one might conclude that these spiritual people are somehow very different from regular people. As for me, I can claim no miracles. I have been a simple person all my life. Early on I learned that if I worked hard, I would usually get good results: nothing supernatural about that.

I was born in 1927 in Sri Lanka, a teardrop-shaped island off the southeast coast of India. It is a beautiful place of lushly forested mountains, rice paddies, and farms of rubber plants and tea trees. My tiny village consisted entirely of a cluster of about forty mud huts and the nearby Buddhist temple, our only public gathering place. No one had electricity or running water.

Nearly everyone in our village was poor, desperately poor. But our Theravada Buddhist belief system gave us unshakeable confidence in life. Our entire village's anchor was the temple. People went there to visit the monks and ask them to chant *suttas,* or Buddhist discourses, for nearly every event: weddings,

Bhante Henepola Gunaratana, 75, a Theravada monk, is the author of Mindfulness in Plain English.

birthdays, serious illness, and deaths. The monks served as teachers, preachers, advisors, and sometimes even as physicians. People also enjoyed simply chatting with the monks at any hour of
the day or night. The temple was always open.

My parents shared a deep devotion to Buddhism. Every morning we children woke up to the sing-song chant of them reading
Pali suttas. These daily recitations served as our lullaby at night,
too. Before we even learned the alphabet, we could recite Pali
devotional stanzas from memory, and we knew what the words
kamma and *rebirth* meant.

───────────

When I was about eight or nine I abruptly lost my night vision,
probably because of malnutrition. After dark, it was as if I were
blind, and I couldn't see anything at all, even with the light from
a kerosene lamp. My mother consulted the village medicine man,
who gave her a bitter-tasting herbal potion for me.

My mother was supposed to grind the herb into a paste and
feed it to me every day until my eyesight improved. The paste
tasted wretched, and to make matters worse, I was supposed to
take this foul concoction early in the morning, when my stomach
was empty. To get me to take that medicine, my mother used the
power of love. Before anyone else in the house was awake, she
would take me onto her lap. She would hug me, kiss me, and tell
me stories in a low whisper. After a few minutes, I was so relaxed
and happy that I would have done anything she asked. That was
the moment she would put the medicine in my mouth and tell me
to swallow it quickly. She always mixed the bitter paste with sugar,
though it still tasted awful. But after several months of that daily
ritual, I completely recovered my eyesight.

Now, many years later, I understand the power of *metta*, or
loving-kindness. In a way, it helps us swallow the bitterness of life.
It smoothes over the rough moments, the disappointments, the

hurt. The Buddha used the power of metta to "conquer" many of his enemies. He even instructed monks living in the forest to use metta when confronted by poisonous snakes. And the Metta Sutta is one of the most beautiful of his discourses. My mother understood and lived the words of the Buddha. She made sure all her children heard stories of the Buddha's life, and learned about his compassion and wisdom. She herself was a walking example of metta, always treating anyone she met with gentleness and soft words. In many ways, I consider her almost a holy person.

———————————

On full-moon and new-moon days, laypeople spent the whole day and night at the temple. Monks from neighboring villages would also come to our temple and would take turns sitting on the throne and delivering sermons. In the evening, a solemn ceremony unfolded. After all the laypeople assembled in the preaching hall, a learned monk was carried in by two men folding their arms together to make a seat. There weren't many of these highly respected monks. Some of them could recite the entire Pali canon by memory, and knew all the commentaries as well. They were skilled in picking apart a discourse and explaining every point, in marathon sermons that lasted as long as ten hours. They were usually renowned for their storytelling abilities and their sweet chanting voices.

The monk was gently lowered into his chair on the platform, then wrapped in a white cloth up to his neck. A curtain was drawn in front of him, leaving only his face showing. The sermon would begin around 8 P.M. Sometimes it would last all night. Children fell asleep on the floor beside their parents. The adults, however, were supposed to stay awake. To help them, an old man with a long white beard sat in front of the platform. Every time the monk paused to take a breath, the old man said very loudly, "YES, Venerable Sir!"

Sometimes I would wake up in the middle of the night and find the whole room asleep, save for the monk and that old man. It amazed me that anyone managed to stay awake. Around 5 A.M., the drum-beaters began thumping a beat, and people would begin to stir. By then the monk had moved into the last part of his sermon, explaining how Maitreya, the future Buddha, will appear when the teachings of Gotama, our present Buddha, are no longer in practice. At 6 A.M., the monk would open the curtain and stretch out his legs, which had been folded in the same position all night. Several men would approach him, carrying a pan of warm coconut oil. For fifteen minutes, they'd massage his feet and legs with the oil. Then the monk would descend from the platform and retire to his room to wash before breakfast.

Watching all this as a young boy, I was deeply impressed. The laypeople's pious attitude and respect for the monk was inspiring. I told my parents that I wanted to become a monk: I wanted to deliver sermons and be carried to my chair by reverent people. Not only that, but I would teach Dhamma in English, I boasted. My oldest brother had taught me the English alphabet, as well as a few English words. Nobody else in our village knew any English at all, even though it was the "official" language of Ceylon under British rule. We villagers were allowed to use Sinhalese, but English was clearly the language of the elite—those with government jobs, those in high society, those wealthy enough to travel. So I thought if I could learn English, I would be the ultimate educated monk.

My parents listened to my childish dreams, and they laughed.

As I grew older, my interest in becoming a monk intensified.

Before I became a bhikkhu, I loved pretending I was a bhikkhu. I would wrap a piece of white cloth around me, the way monks wrap their robes around them, and sit down under a tree in the forest. I imagined that the other trees around me were people, and I preached to the crowd of silent listeners, reciting a few Pali stanzas I'd heard at the temple. I would also sit and pretend to be deep in "meditation," though I had no idea what meditation was.

Even then, I believed it was somehow my kamma to become a monk. This is not to say that it was my "fate" to be a monk, for Buddhism has no such notions. Rather, because of all the accumulated causes and conditions in my past, however long that may be, I now wanted to be a Buddhist monk. Perhaps I had been a monk in a previous life—not a totally successful one, because I obviously didn't achieve enlightenment in that life, but not a complete failure, either, because I had the good fortune to be reborn as a human being, with another chance to better myself spiritually. But even putting such notions aside, the impulse to ordain and that deep longing to wear the saffron robe flowered in me very early.

By the time I was eleven years old, I had lost interest in the boyhood mischief and pranks my brother and I used to enjoy, but I'd also lost interest in school. I wanted only to enter the two-and-a-half-millennia-old order of Buddhist monks, in the ancient Asian tradition. Stories of young boys in the time of the Buddha who had had similar aspirations to become monks captivated me. I was steadfast in pursuit of my goal. I pestered my parents about becoming a bhikkhu long enough that they gradually began to take my request more seriously, as something more than a passing whim. I was still too young to ordain fully, but I could live in a temple and train as a novice. It was considered very auspicious for a family if one of its sons entered the order.

So, with some reluctance, my father finally agreed to let me try temple life. My mother cried because she hated to see me leave home, but she saw in my determination that it was inevitable—

my birth horoscope had even predicted it! My father consulted the village astrologer to determine a lucky day for me to leave home. In those days, astrology dictated the main events of our lives. People consulted the stars for deciding when to plant a crop, when to marry, when to cremate the dead, when to cut a child's hair for the first time, when to start an important job, even when to dig the foundation for a building. Although astrological principles may seem contrary to the Buddha's teaching of kammic law of cause and effect, belief in astrology coexisted nonetheless alongside Buddhist practices and no one thought this was a problem in the least.

While I was eating the milk rice my mother had prepared for my home-leaving day, I saw that tears were beginning to roll down the cheeks of my mother and sisters. And my brother was trying to hold back his tears. As the time to leave approached, my father appeared, dressed in his best white sarong and shirt. He told me it was time to get going. I put on a white sarong and shirt, too.

By then my brother was crying openly, and suddenly it became very hard to leave. Mixed feelings swirled into a knot in my throat. I was happy to at last be going to a temple, but I was very sad to leave my family. With this departure I was symbolically renouncing home life to take up what is called "the homeless life," the life of a Buddhist monk. The family gathered in front of the house to see me off. I knelt before my mother and touched my forehead to the sand at her feet. She stroked my head with both of her hands.

"May the Triple Gem protect you," she murmured, her voice thick and choked. "May all the gods protect you. May you live long in good health. May no harm come to you."

And then she started sobbing.

I stood up and she kissed my forehead and gave me a strong hug.

My father and I walked many hours along dusty roads to

reach the temple that would be my new home. We had no appointment, and my father had not told the temple I was coming. The stars said it was an auspicious day for my home-leaving, and that was that.

Life at the temples where I studied was hard. I had many duties assigned to me. I was to split firewood for cooking, bring water from the well, sweep the grounds, pick flowers for the altar, cook, wash dishes, and feed the dozen dogs and cats that roamed the temple compound. Between chores I was supposed to be memorizing Sanskrit stanzas from books called *Sataka,* which literally means "one hundred" but generally refers to one hundred verses composed in praise of the Buddha. When we memorized all of one book, we moved on to another. One of the Sataka books explains the one hundred and eight names of the Buddha, another presents the nine admirable qualities of the Buddha, and so on. The purpose of forcing young boys to memorize those stanzas was threefold: to teach us correct Sanskrit pronunciation, to introduce us to the qualities of the Buddha, and most importantly, I think, to arouse faith and devotion in our young minds.

At one temple I stayed at, each evening, as we recited our day's memorizations, the head monk would turn the kerosene lamp very low so that I couldn't cheat by reading my texts. If I made mistakes or hadn't memorized enough verses, he would get angry and slap me. Usually, though, I did well at the recitations. I seemed to be a quick learner, and my teacher was pleased. Within three months, he announced that I had progressed well and was ready for novice ordination.

After ordination, I eventually enrolled at a monks' school. Very quickly I became known as the smartest student in the school. I discovered I had a photographic memory—clearly a gift of good kamma. In ten minutes, I could read a long book and retain everything in it. I don't know how this worked; I just know that each page stuck in my mind like a picture. I was very proud of my gift and told my friends to challenge me by asking questions from books. I could answer them with the page number, and even the punctuation, of the sentence in question.

Perhaps because of this, the principal of the school liked me, and selected me to be his assistant. Because of my privileges and responsibilities, several of my fellow monks became jealous of me, and it didn't help that I had developed the habit of reporting other students' weaknesses to the principal! In short, I was a rat. I filed report after report, detailing the wrongdoings of other monks. I knew that I should be more concerned with my own behavior than with finding faults in others, but I wanted so much to maintain the approval of the principal.

It's too bad that I didn't take to heart the words of the Buddha in the Dhammapada:

> Easily seen is the fault of others, but one's own is difficult to see.
>
> Like chaff, one winnows another's faults but hides one's own, even as a crafty fowler hides behind sham branches. He who seeks another's faults, who is ever censorious, his cankers grow. He is far from destruction of the cankers.

―――――――――

When I was fifteen or so, I became interested in a village girl about my age. Every day she would stand in front of her house as I came by with the alms bowl. She was near my height, with long black hair. She had a round face like mine, with skin lighter than the normal Sinhalese complexion, and a perfect set of teeth that showed whenever she smiled. I thought she was beautiful. One day, as she ladled rice into my bowl, we had a very brief, whispered conversation very much against the monastic rules.

That evening, when I went to our well to take a bath, I deliberately banged the bucket against the sides of the well to make a noise loud enough for her to hear at her house. Within moments she ran to the well, carrying a pot as if she needed to fill it with water. For about ten days, that was our routine. Even though we were too shy to share our budding feelings for each other, we had long, lovely conversations, and each time they got longer and longer. Eventually my teacher began to wonder why I was taking so long at my bath and one day he came to check on me, and caught us there.

Of course he was upset. Monks of any age are not supposed to have close contact with females. He ordered the girl not to come to the well when I was there. Back at the temple, he reprimanded me in very strong language and ordered me to take my baths later at night—a time he thought would be too late for her to come to the well. Actually, that suited me fine because I knew we would have even more privacy to talk after dark, when no one would see us together. So we continued our clandestine meetings.

Inevitably, my teacher caught us again, and this time his rebuke was even more harsh. He told the girl never to come to the well again. He said that he was going to report her behavior to her parents. She cried and begged him not to tell her parents. She promised not to go to the well anymore and she didn't. I never saw her again.

When I look back on that incident now, after years of Dhamma study and practice, I see it as evidence that boys perhaps should not be ordained so young, as was customary in my childhood. They should first receive a secular education and be allowed to enjoy games, sports, friends, and parties—all the things that young people crave. Then, when they have grown into adults, they can make a mature decision about whether to be ordained. Joining the Sangha is a serious commitment, and I don't think a very young person is prepared to make an informed choice about it. And it would be a rare boy who was emotionally ready to cope with the rigors and restrictions of monastic life.

The traditional thinking in my country was that boys, with their vigorous young minds, could memorize sacred texts more easily. Their personalities could be shaped and molded early into the peaceful demeanor of a contemplative monk. But now I'm not so sure that's true. I have seen plenty of men who became monks in middle or old age, after being married and having raised children, and they make fine bhikkhus. And I've seen too many monks, on the other hand, who were ordained before puberty who continue to behave like children.

Just before turning twenty, I received my higher monk's ordination. A few days after the ceremony, I eagerly took on one of the privileges of a full monk to participate in a seven-day chanting. This ritual, called *paritta* in Pali, is designed to drive away evil spirits. If someone is sick or if a village is suffering from famine or drought (misfortunes that potentially could be the doing of evil spirits), people ask monks to perform this special chanting. For an entire week, pairs of monks chant nonstop. Each pair chants for an hour at a time and are then relieved by another pair. The chanting is energetic—more like shouting than singing. Only monks with strong chanting voices are selected, and they are held in high esteem for their efforts. Young monks impatiently wait their turn to join the chanting teams.

One of my friends from monks' school was as eager as I to participate in a chanting. We wrangled an invitation to participate in a chant from a friend of ours who was head monk at a temple nearby. We were young and enthusiastic, and since this was our first seven-day chanting, we wanted more than just one turn. So my friend and I begged some of the older monks to give us their slots. They had already done many parittas and were happy to oblige, so we ended up chanting most of the time. Our only breaks were for eating and answering the call of nature. We didn't sleep at all!

Each day at 6 A.M., 11 A.M., and 6 P.M., drummers would announce the start of devotional services by beating on drums. They had to beat loudly to be heard over our chanting. To prove our zeal, my friend and I only chanted louder. Trying to drown out the drums, we were eventually shouting at the top of our lungs. After three days my friend passed out. Some of the laypeople at the temple took him to a bedroom and laid him on a bed to sleep. By evening he recovered, and joined me again in the chanting.

By the end of the week, we were both in bad shape. Even though we desperately needed rest, we couldn't sleep. We couldn't eat, either, and both of us had severe headaches. We couldn't stand to be around anyone else, and I think we must have been suffering some kind of nervous breakdown.

Worst of all, I lost my memory—and not just my photographic memory, everything! I couldn't recognize any alphabet, Sinhalese, Sanskrit, Tamil, or English. I would open a book and be unable to make any sense of what was on the page. If I met someone and then saw him five minutes later, I couldn't remember his name. I was angry and upset and humbled by what had happened to me. All my pride in my academic achievements was gone. Back at school, I failed my final exams. The principal, puzzled why his star pupil had done so miserably, called me into his office. I told him about the seven-day chanting and how my memory had disappeared. He told me to go back to my temple to rest and get some treatment.

After a month I was no better, but I yearned to return to school, nonetheless. My glory days were over. I now had to struggle to learn even the simplest things. Some nights, while reading a textbook, I felt like insects were running all over my scalp. I was in agony and began to entertain thoughts of suicide. I didn't want to live in that condition at all. I had heard that the fabric mantels in kerosene lamps were poisonous if you ate them, so I started collecting them and hiding them in a box. Luckily, my friends got wind of my plan and threw the box away.

For most of the next year I subjected myself to all kinds of treatments in a desperate search for a "cure." I saw an Ayurvedic doctor; monks (ironically) did an all-night chanting for me to chase away an evil spirit; my parents called on an exorcist, and then invited an even more powerful one when he didn't work; and last of all my teacher gave me a talisman to wear around my neck. None of this worked.

At this point of utter desperation a very unusual thought occurred to me: perhaps meditation would help. When my friends heard that plan, they burst out laughing. The practice of meditation was hardly a common thing to do in those days, even for a bhikkhu.

"Are you crazy?" my friends said. "Meditation is only for old people who can't do anything else anymore. You're still too young to meditate. Don't be foolish."

Although I was well-versed in the theory of meditation and knew the four foundations of mindfulness by heart, I had never actually meditated, believe it or not. Very few monks did, in those days. They were too busy preaching Dhamma, chanting, and performing blessing ceremonies. There was much talk about meditation, of course, but very little practice. Some people actually believed that if a person meditated too much, it would cause mental disturbance. Well, I figured, I already had a mental disturbance. What did I have to lose?

Secretly I began to meditate sometimes late at night, sometimes early in the morning. Whenever I could steal a few minutes alone, I meditated, sitting in a dark corner of the shrine room where I hoped nobody would notice me. I knew I was trying to instill a new mental habit and in order to be successful, I had to set aside time every day to do it. It was like a workout for the mind, trying to flex muscles that were weak from lack of training. At first, I simply tried to calm my mind by recalling mundane things—names of my friends or temples I had visited, titles of books I'd read. It wasn't easy; there were big gaps in my memory. But I tried not to panic. Then, drawing on my scriptural training in the four foundations of mindfulness, I began to watch the flow of breath, of bodily sensations, feelings, and thoughts that moved through me. That watchful observance gradually led to a very peaceful feeling inside. Occasionally I even experienced spontaneous flashes of joy. Those brief moments, of course, made meditation enjoyable and encouraged me to keep going.

Eventually, things I had studied in the past started coming back to me. I began to recognize letters and numbers. Unexpectedly, my temper, too, began to improve. After a couple of months of steady practice, I was able to read again and to remember what I had read. I was elated, and so relieved that I had found a "cure." Meditation did what all the incantations and medicinal oils and talismans hadn't been able to do. It brought peace to my mind.

I can say that whenever I was arrogant in my life, I suffered a great deal. As a young man in monks' college, I spied on other students, I gossiped, I was always looking for others' faults and because of that, I was miserable. In fact, I'd say that has always been my greatest weakness: finding fault in others. Rising above that defilement even a little bit took many long years, through much trial and error, and even now I occasionally struggle with it. But more or less nowadays, I'm happy to say, I can pretty much accept people as they are. And my life (not to mention theirs!) is so much smoother as a result.

By relying on the Buddha's teachings, I have learned slowly to withdraw from conflict rather than charging into it or, worse still, going looking for it. That, too, has made life immeasurably more peaceful. With the help of the Buddha's teachings and the practice of mindfulness, the greatest change I have made in myself, I think, is that I can easily forgive people now, no matter what they do—and believe me, this skill didn't come easily! I had to work long and hard at it. But my own anger, contentiousness, and judgmentalness were fertile ground for practice. Just because a person becomes a monk, by no means is he immediately free from all defilements of character or empty of worldly concerns.

As a monk, I have dedicated my life to protecting and maintaining the Buddha's teaching. I have found that because of that, the Dhamma has protected and maintained me as well. That's what I have learned in my seventy-five years. The Dhamma was and is my shield, my umbrella in the worst storms. It's a shelter we can always rely on, if we simply remember to. I hope you will find that shelter in your life, as well.

SECTION IV
Looking Ahead

When I was a teenager, I picked Philip Kapleau's classic *The Three Pillars of Zen* off our bookshelves at home. It was one of the first books my dad had read in the early '70s, when he was a young man learning meditation. I skimmed through the Dharma talks and instructions on proper posture, almost ready to put the book down. Then I came to the section that had personal stories of *kensho*, or enlightenment, resulting from sitting meditation intensively in retreat. The stories were vivid. That kensho could happen to an ordinary lay person—a housewife, a schoolteacher—told me that one did not need to be special to do this. I read them over and over again. I was especially captivated by the private letters between a Zen master and a Japanese woman in her early twenties. She was in the process of dying, and used her remaining time, under the guidance of the Zen master, to reach deeper and deeper stages of awakening. That a young person, and a woman, could advance so far left a deep impression on me. These personal stories took Buddhism from an abstract philosophy to a lived, immediate practice.

I became inspired to listen to narratives from others, and from then on often asked people to tell me how they got started and how

Buddhism changed their lives. I learned much about the realities and challenges of the Buddhist path. In my early twenties, I became interested in the spiritual lives of young people like myself.

Through hundreds of small conversations and interactions accumulated over these last seven years in searching for my generation, and also through my own experience as a young Buddhist, three issues have come to light. First, young Buddhists today are searching for communities of like-minded people, young and older, for support and guidance. They do not always find it nor are they always made to feel welcome. Second, many young Buddhists are eager to take on active, participatory roles in Dharma organizations, either through career choices or volunteering. Yet the many options available to young people are not widely known or offered. Third, young people come into the Dharma with big metaphysical questions as well as daily-life and psychological concerns. In many cases, teachers and others are not familiar with how to address these immediate concerns about relationships, family, maturity, education, and so on.

In this section, I would like to explore the dimensions of these three issues to consider how the Buddhist community at large can nurture and support the spiritual lives of its young people.

But before diving in, I want to acknowledge that this discussion applies primarily to the Western American Buddhist communities in the Zen, Vajrayana, and Theravada traditions. Other communities, notably the Jodo Shinshu (domestically), the Soka Gakkai International-USA (SGI-USA), and many of the Asian American temples, have established programs for their younger members. Likewise, in the last ten or so years, temples in Asia have taken a proactive stance to working with young Buddhists. In fact, it might be of tremendous benefit for the Western American Buddhists to take a look at what these other groups are doing. I think of the temporary ordination program in Korea, an idea they've imported from the Theravada tradition in Southeast Asia, in which young people can try out being a monk or nun for a week. Could we arrange similar programs here in the U.S. in some of the *vipassana* centers? There's much to learn from these more well-established communities about nurturing and developing a successor generation.

COMMUNITY SUPPORT

A year ago, I went to a Buddhist youth conference in Seoul, South Korea. It was a mostly pan-Asian youth conference, and I was the only youth representative from the Western Hemisphere. The conference was held in a luxury hotel, which created a business-like atmosphere. The youth representatives, some as young as nineteen, from Indonesia, Thailand, Malaysia, India, Taiwan, and so on, were all dressed in business suits. The young women had pretty scarves tied around their necks, their hair pulled back in buns. The representatives sat along a long table on the stage, and as the panel got underway, each flipped open a laptop to begin PowerPoint presentations about the Buddhist youth groups in their countries. The presentations were sophisticated, with music from *Star Wars* and other hits accompanying screens of diagrams and statistics. Older Buddhists—monks, nuns, parents, and devout laypeople—who had organized and funded the event, watched proudly as each youth representative reported on the many activities of Buddhist organizations in their home country.

At first, I was put off by the stiffness and formality of the whole scene. It seemed like these young Buddhists didn't have a strong heart connection to Buddhism. Few were talking about awakening, freedom, insight, self-transformation, or social action. I sat listening to one speech after another, struggling to find something personally valuable in the conference.

As the conference progressed, though, I began sensing that there was actually something very wonderful going on. It was subtle but powerful. I saw that the youth had strong bonds of friendship among each other. They had met several times before in different countries to learn about the Buddhism of that country. Between tours, they stayed in touch through email and instant messaging. Now reunited, they had invented a group cheer and a language among themselves. They played games, flirted, gossiped, and moved around in groups. There was a sense of togetherness and companionship. It seemed they were there as much for the friendships as they were for the Buddhism. Sharing a religion and values was essential to forming their identity as committed Buddhists. Embracing this lovely group of cheerful young Buddhists was a larger group of older Buddhists, who shepherded us from one fun place to another. The older Buddhists looked on with encouragement, taking photos, chatting, and creating a supportive social atmosphere.

I suddenly felt envious. This kind of nurturing atmosphere was something I had longed for as a teenager and college student. I wasn't even aware that I had missed it until I saw what could be. I began wishing that Western Americans could do better about creating community and inter-generational support. It seems to me that despite the cultural differences between the Asian youth and the Western American youth, as youth we all feel a strong need to belong. Many of the young Buddhists in America say that they are searching for community, that they feel isolated and alone. Unfortunately, because America is such a big country, Buddhists tend to live far apart. Even those who live near a center often find it is focused on the practice of meditation, which is an internal, relatively non-social activity. Moreover, whatever social life does exist in a Dharma center is often geared towards the majority of older members. For example, here is a posting from a teenager on Beliefnet.com's teen Buddhist discussion group:

> I have a question that's been concerning me for a while now. I finally found a meditation group to meditate and share the Buddha's teachings with, but there's one problem; they're all adults and I'm the only young person there. It feels kind of awkward when I'm there because there is no-one my age there. I am afraid that they think I'm a stupid teenager just looking to try something different instead of looking for a spiritual path. What should I do to solve this inner turmoil of mine?

And here is one of the responses from another teen:

> Don't worry; all the Buddhists I know (aside from the Internet) are also adults. There's a temple near where I live that I plan to go to soon, and they don't have any young people! Look at it this way: if they shun or judge you for being young, they aren't practicing Buddhism very well, are they? :)

In Asia, and in many Asian-American temples, teenage Buddhist youth rarely feel out of place, since many of the temples have youth groups and activities for families and young adults.

In college, I was briefly part of the campus Christian fellowship, since no student Buddhist group existed at the time. I delighted in the strong sense of togetherness that the fellowship provided. The community was a safe environment for us to learn from each other, to talk about values and ways of living, to explore our thoughts on the meaning of life, and to reflect on how what we were learning in the classroom applied to our lives. Christian groups in general seemed to have recognized that young adults rely on community as they make the not-always-easy transition from their parents' homes to independence. The tribal-like system that the Intervarsity Christian Fellowship, an evangelical, national organization, sets up on campuses is especially effective in supporting and retaining their members. I am not suggesting that Buddhism in America follow their model exactly. However, it seems to me that Buddhist groups might do well to foster a more supportive, family-like atmosphere in welcoming and nurturing young people. This is not so much to recruit young Buddhists as it is to support the ones who are beginning to explore the path.

Looking ahead, I hope older Buddhists will not be shy about offering their presence, kindness, perspective, and care to the young seekers around them. Many of the essays in this anthology reveal how the support of seasoned practitioners is integral to development: the parents of Hilary Miller, Maya Putra, Tenzin Youdon, Alexis Trass, and Bhiksuni Thich Chan Chau Nghiem; the masters of Sumana Bhikkhu and Jimmy Yu; the *bodhisattva* friend of J. Marion. Experienced Buddhists have a tremendous amount to offer in mentoring younger Buddhists—and they need not be big-time Dharma teachers to do it! For their part, I hope young Buddhists will not be dismissive of the years of experience residing in the older generation. Perhaps in the near future there can be greater inter-generational connection of the kind that I found at the conference in Seoul.

COMMUNITY ROLES

At Wesleyan University, there is a dormitory called Buddhist House. It was formerly a huge frat, but now the main living room is set up as a meditation hall with a shrine. This past fall, the house had a weekend retreat called "Interdependence: Buddhism for Our Generation," led by two under-thirty Shambhala students. The poster read:

> Is Buddhism actually *relevant* to the 21st century? Or is it just the latest attempt by our consumer culture to commodify something foreign and exotic? *What's the point* of meditation? What does it have to do with my life? What does Buddhism have to say about *politics* and the anti-war movement? About activism in general? About the media? About *living a meaningful life* in a materialistic world? Do you have to run away from the world and become a nun to understand yourself? And what the hell are you wearing those beads for? This weekend will focus on the issues that face our generation as we explore meditation practice and Buddhist teachings.

I was impressed that Buddhist House and the retreat had been organized by young Buddhists themselves. The home-designed posters brought more than forty people together, including some older Buddhists, for the weekend.

Perhaps the organizers were on to something in assessing that "youth attracts youth," that an effective way of drawing in young people is to have other young people out in front. In several other instances, in the last few years, young Buddhists have been increasingly taking the initiative to energize other young people. Most are mentored by older Buddhists who provide valuable guidance in creating unique pathways to make the Dharma accessible to a wide range of others. For example, Noah Levine and Brad Warner have written about how punk and rebellion can be a springboard for Dharma practice. Soren Gordhamer and others bring yoga and meditation into juvenile halls. Bhiksuni Thich Chan Chau Nghiem and Viveka Chen are helping arrange retreats for young people of color. Diana Winston has published a meditation book for teenagers. Recently, Buddhist college groups banded together to form the Buddhist Student Network, which helps leaders navigate the complexities of starting and maintaining a college group.

But I also meet a lot of young people who want to actively participate in Dharma community, but who aren't sure what is possible, either as a career or as an extracurricular. Young Buddhists, and actually older ones, too, sometimes limit their thinking about roles to that of "The Dharma Teacher." Yet, when I look at Asia, I'm struck by the diversity of positions that have allowed the tradition to thrive from one generation to the next. Monastics, after initial training, specialize as scholars, public intellectuals, apologists and theologians, chaplains, social workers, administrators, finance overseers, liturgists, ascetic nirvana-obtainers, pilgrimage guides, political advisors, artists, dancers, musicians, and more. In the West, we do not have a sizable monastic class that can fulfill these functions. But, would it be possible to direct young Buddhists to take up positions similar to those established in Asia?

Perhaps we are coming upon a time in which we can have clearly laid-out pathways in any number of Buddhist vocations for our youth. Here are just a few examples. As Dharma organizations become more established they are developing specific professional needs (especially in financial management) in administration. A young person could be advised to consider a degree in non-profit management and even be offered scholarship support. Or, a certificate in copyediting would allow someone to work on the manuscripts from Buddhist publishing houses. Training in Buddhist chaplaincy opens opportunities for counseling in hospitals, hospices, international shipping ports, and the military. If we can be imaginative about cultivating leadership roles for our youth, then these can focus and energize young Buddhists.

PSYCHOLOGICAL SUPPORT

The Dharma center where I now work has changed a lot in just six years. When I first worked here, there were hardly any young people. Today, there are many twenty- and thirty-somethings on the staff. It has been wonderful to see this recent upsurge of young people investing themselves in the Dharma path, a reflection of a broader trend across the U.S. Among the young staff, the central and vibrantly discussed question is, "What am I doing with my life and how does Dharma practice fit into it all?"

On a recent afternoon, Jon Kabat-Zinn, a prominent figure on the Dharma scene, was a guest speaker for the staff meeting. (Kabat-Zinn started the Mindfulness Based Stress Reduction Center, which has made a secular form of mindfulness meditation popular in hospitals, schools, and other non-religious institutions.) One of the staff persons, aged twenty-four, asked Kabat-Zinn that vibrantly discussed question about figuring out our lives.

Kabat-Zinn replied that the first thing was to be patient. "I was as old as twenty-seven when I got my doctorate and I didn't even begin what became my life's work until I was thirty-five. It's good to drop back into the moment and let things unfold. This is where Dharma practice, which teaches us how to live in the present moment, is useful." At the same time, he said, it's important to try things out, "get bruised, get knocked down, be disappointed, get in there and get dirty" to see what you really want to do. "You might go through a not-this, not-that phase as you do different jobs. Then, someday, it will suddenly become clear to you what you should do with your life, your talents. It will unfold without your effort." The young staff nodded in agreement. It was reassuring to know that someone as successful as Kabat-Zinn had had his own years of searching before finding his purpose in the world.

The moment pointed to the need for young adults to receive advice and perspective appropriate to their stage in life. One of the major projects ahead for Dharma teachers may be to produce material specific to the questions of the young adult years. Much of the Dharma literature is directed towards older age groups, most of which is still useful to younger people. However, there are some questions common to most young adults that perhaps could be best addressed directly.

In a retreat for college students a year ago, a teacher and I asked the students to write down something they were having difficulty with, a question or challenge. The notes were anonymous and placed in a large box in the center of the circle. I pulled notes out randomly, read them aloud to the group, and then we discussed the problems in light of Buddhist practice. Here are some samples from that group:

A friend of mine started dating my ex-boyfriend and I'm so mad that I don't know how to practice loving-kindness towards her.

I've been impatient with myself lately: I'm young and know that I have many years ahead of me but I find that I judge myself when I can't get everything done that I want to.

How can I learn to take care of myself when I'm in university?

What if friends or family members don't have the same values as you do?

In relationships, being fully and openly loving without clinging or selfish desiring—how do you do it?

I was struck that these students were asking very personal, direct questions about their everyday lives. The questions were not philosophical, not about the meaning of life or the nature of suffering. While the students were also thinking about very large questions such as "Who am I?" and "How can I become free?" they needed to talk about much more immediate issues. They wanted to know how Buddhism could address these questions, how Dharma speaks to the practical and spiritual dimensions of growing up.

Some other questions I often hear among young Buddhists are:

How do I tell my parents about what I'm doing? How should I handle their reaction?

How do I perform daily practice in a university setting?

What is the balance between inner spiritual cultivation and outer worldly action? I.e., should I go on retreats or get a job?

Is it okay to shop among different Buddhisms, and how do I know I've found the right one?

I'm feeling lost and in transition: how can Dharma help me?

How can I survive stress at school?

What does Buddhism have to say about living ethically (with regard to abortion, pre-marital sex, intoxicants, cheating, revenge, working in the military, betraying a friend)?

I am not certain that Buddhist communities have developed teachings that are responsive to these kinds of questions. Some young people have talked about moments in which a Buddhist teacher gave an impossibly abstract answer or an instruction that would be difficult to put into practice, such as "everything is empty" or "practice non-attachment."

Recently, I asked Franz Metcalf, who wrote the wonderful book *Buddha in Your Backpack,* one of the only books to begin answering the kinds of questions that young adults have, what motivated him to write it. He said that he remembers his teen years as being the most spiritually connected and probing time in his life, but that he was not given sufficient frameworks for thinking about the kind of experiences he was having. He wanted to provide teenagers a way to deal with the already natural spirituality that they were experiencing. In my view, we need to hear more from potential mentors and Dharma teachers in the way that Franz has articulated. For example, a visit to the teen discussion board on Beliefnet.com reveals a rich and wonderful dialogue among the teenagers. However, some of the postings are alarming, with a few teenagers in considerable distress. Part of me feels the urge to step in and provide some support where the other respondents are at a loss. In a way, I could see the non-dominating presence of a Buddhist chaplain being very helpful, in this and in many other settings.

Dharma teachers in the West have said that they do not have sufficient skills in the psychological arts when it comes to their students and sometimes must rely on some professional assistance from counselors and psychiatrists. Some Dharma teachers are reluctant to work with youth because the psychology of young adults seems too different from most other, older students. It may be that those who work with youth need to know something about child, teen, and young-adult psychology, and learn how to respond both compassionately and wisely to the suffering of our young-adult population. As you yourself have probably experienced, one sees the value of a religion when it begins to make us happier, more wholesome people. If we give abstract Buddhist answers to young adults when they're asking immediate, practical questions—like, how can I relate to my disapproving parents?—then young adults might lose interest in Dharma. In order to receive the next generation skillfully, it may be time for teachers and mentors to develop basic counseling skills or have training in youth-specific needs.

LOOKING AHEAD

In the last several years, Buddhist communities have seen a small but noticeable wave of newcomers, many of them middle-aged but just as many who are young. Recently, I looked in on a weekend retreat for beginners. How moving to see each student wholeheartedly learning meditation! The retreat had so many applicants that a second beginner's retreat was scheduled, at the last minute, for another weekend. Buddhist groups on college campuses are also being visited more frequently from curious, but not yet committed, students.

How are we, the greater Buddhist community in America, going to receive these beginners and young people? Some attention is needed if we want to cultivate a generation to which we can confidently pass on the profound teachings of Buddhism. I hope we will all, young and older alike, continue to develop a welcoming atmosphere in our individual communities, in magazines and online forums, in events, and so on. If we create some participatory roles, this will energize young people. I hope young people themselves continue to take the initiative in being creative and active. Perhaps most importantly, we need to consider how to respond to the specific psychological needs of teenagers and young adults. Addressing these three areas will be essential to supporting not just the newcomers, but those young people, such as the writers in this anthology, who have already practiced Buddhism for some years.

In the last seven years, I have come to see that there is a vast potential reservoir of care, support, and experience in the collective Buddhist communities, in all generations, and in the resources of monastics, Dharma teachers, parents, and laypeople. I hope we will begin to more consciously offer these resources to the next generation.

Glossary

AMIDA (AMITABHA) BUDDHA: (Japanese) an important buddha of the Mahayana, especially the Pure Land school, who symbolizes mercy and wisdom.

BHIKKHU (BHIKSHUS): (Pali) a monk, a male member of the Buddhist sangha who has entered homelessness and received full ordination.

BODHICITTA: (Sanskrit) the aspiration to achieve enlightenment for the benefit of all sentient beings.

BODHISATTVA: (Sanskrit) one who aspires to buddhahood for oneself and all beings.

CHAN: Chinese for "Zen."

CIRCUMAMBULATE: (English) to walk clockwise around a sacred site, thereby creating good karma or merit.

DAIMOKU: (Japanese) literally "title," that is, the title of the Lotus Sutra, *Nam-myoho-renge-kyo*.

DANA: (Sanskrit) generosity or the act of giving.

DHAMMAPADA: (Pali) 426 verses on the basics of the Buddhist teaching, popular in Theravada Buddhism.

DHARMA/DHAMMA: (Sanskrit/Pali) the teachings of the Buddha.

DUKKHA: (Sanskrit) suffering; the unsatisfactory quality that marks existence.

DZOGCHEN: (Tibetan) lit., "the great perfection," a tradition that asserts that the mind is already pure and needs only to be recognized as such.

GATHA: (Sanskrit) brief Buddhist songs or poems.

GOHONZON: (Japanese) the mandala that serves as the object of devotion in Nichiren Buddhism and is the embodiment of the law of *Nam-myoho-renge-kyo.*

GOTAMA: another name for the Buddha.

JATAKA TALES: (Pali) stories detailing the previous lives of the Buddha.

JODO SHINSHU (SHIN BUDDHISM): (Japanese) lit. "True School of the Pure Land." A school of Japanese Buddhism founded by Shinran (1173–1262) that venerates Amida Buddha.

KENSHO: (Japanese) expression in Zen for seeing one's own true nature, or the experience of awakening.

KOAN: (Japanese) a teaching tool of the Rinzai Zen school used to stimulate insight, often seeming to take the form of a riddle or paradoxical proposition that cannot be solved by rational thinking.

KUAN YIN: Chinese version of Avalokiteshvara, the great bodhisattva of compassion.

LAMA: (Tibetan) a religious master or guru.

MAHAYANA: (Sanskrit) the "great vehicle" of Buddhism that emphasizes the bodhisattva path and salvation of all beings.

MAITREYA: (Sanskrit) the future Buddha, important especially in the Mahayana, who embodies compassion and who presides over Tushita heaven.

MALA: (Sanskrit) a string of beads, often 108 in number, used to count repetitions of the recitation of mantras, certain chants, and the name of Buddha.

MANTRA: (Sanskrit) syllables, often Sanskrit, recited to invoke aspects of buddhas, induce purification or insight, grant protection, and so forth.

METTA: (Pali) loving-kindness: the sincere wish for beings to be happy and safe.

NAM-MYOHO-RENGE-KYO: the mantra of Nichiren Buddhism (which is the title of the Lotus Sutra in Japanese) that is identified as the ultimate reality or fundamental law of life.

NEMBUTSU: (Japanese) recitation of the name of Buddha Amida (or Amitabha), a practice of the Pure Land school (Jodoshu), and the True Pure Land school (Jodo Shinshu).

NICHIREN: 1222–82, founder of the Nichiren school of Japanese Buddhism, whose teachings were based on the Lotus Sutra.

NOBLE SILENCE: practice of holding silence by restraining contact with others.

PARITTA: (Pali) a ritual designed to drive away evil spirits.

PURE LAND: buddha-realms or heavens, important to the Mahayana tradition. Also refers to the Pure Land school founded in 402 in China, later brought to Japan by Honen.

ROSHI: (Japanese) title for a senior Zen master.

SANGHA: (Sanskrit) traditionally refers to the community of Buddhist monastics, but can refer to any community of Buddhist practitioners.

SATORI: (Japanese) Zen term for enlightenment; sometimes synonymous with *kensho*.

SOKA GAKKAI: modern Buddhist movement in Japan, whose doctrine is rooted in the thought of Nichiren.

THANGKA: in Tibetan Buddhism, a scroll with a Buddhist painting.

THERAVADA: (Pali) a school of Buddhism, known as the "Way of the Elders"; widespread in Southeast Asia; in America, closely related to the practice of *vipassana,* or insight, meditation.

TRIPLE GEM: the three jewels of Buddhism consisting of the Buddha, Dharma, and Sangha.

VINAYA: (Pali) the monastic code that regulates the conduct and community of monks and nuns.

VIPASSANA: (Pali) insight into the true nature of existence. Also denotes a form of meditation.

ZABUTON: (Japanese) mat on which one practices meditation.

ZAFU: (Japanese) round cushion used for sitting meditation.

ZAZEN: (Japanese) sitting meditation; literally, "sitting Zen."

ZENDO: (Japanese) Zen hall in which meditation is practiced.

Contributors

The essays in this volume were written over a period of four years. For the younger writers especially, much has changed since they wrote their essays. The biographies below are from March 2004 and earlier.

Ajahn Keerati Chatkaew is a Theravada monk in Lodi, California. He was born in the Lampang province of northern Thailand. He received his monastic training at Buddhist University in Bangkok and came to the United States in 1994. Since 1996, he has been mentoring Thai-, Laotian, and Cambodian-American youth in high-crime areas of Stockton, California.

Viveka Chen is a second-generation Chinese American. She was ordained into the Western Buddhist Order (WBO) in 1997 when she was twenty-nine. She is a meditation and Dharma teacher at the San Francisco Buddhist Center (SFBC) of the WBO and since 2000 has served as chairwoman of the Center. Viveka has been working for social and environmental justice in the San Francisco Bay Area's communities of color since 1991. She is also a leader in making meditation available and accessible to people of color and activists. Viveka, one of thirteen teachers at the 2004 Asian American & Pacific Islander Dharma Retreat and Conference sponsored by Spirit Rock Meditation Center, regularly contributes to *Dharma Life* Buddhist magazine and has an essay on the third noble truth coming out in a book for people of color exploring Buddhism.

Phillip Cryan lives in Ames, Iowa, with his fiancée Julia. He returned to the U.S. in November 2003 from Colombia, where he worked for Witness for Peace. He is a free-lance writer writing a biweekly column on media for *Colombia Week* in the meantime. He has practiced primarily in the Chan tradition of Ven. Master Hsuan Hua and the Thai forest tradition of Ajahn Chah, and participated in the Buddhist Alliance for Social Engagement (BASE) program and Zen Hospice Project. Before finding a home in political struggle, he wrote an undergraduate thesis at UC-Berkeley on poststructuralist theory's flirtations with *anatta*. He is working on a book, *News from the Southern Front*, about U.S. intervention in Colombia (to be published by Common Courage Press).

Tenzin Dorjee graduated from Tibetan Children's Village, Dharamsala, in 1998, and from Brown University in 2003. Currently working at the National Endowment for Democracy, Washington, D.C., he is also on the board of directors of Students for a Free Tibet. He is working on a small and simple Buddhist novel.

Zoketsu Norman Fischer was born in Wilkes-Barre, Pennsylvania, in 1946. A Zen priest and poet, he is a former abbot of the San Francisco Zen Center. He is founder and teacher for the Everyday Zen Foundation (www.everydayzen.org), a sangha dedicated to sharing Zen teaching and practice with the world. His latest book, published in 2003 by

HarperSanFrancisco, is *Taking Our Places: The Buddhist Path to Truly Growing Up.*

Bhante G. at age 25.

Bhante Henepola Gunaratana, ordained as a boy in his native Sri Lanka, has been a Buddhist monk for sixty-five of his seventy-five years. He is the abbot of Bhavana Society, a monastery/retreat center in West Virginia that he founded in 1988, but more often than not he's on the road, teaching Dhamma and leading meditation retreats in Europe, Asia, Australia, and South America. Bhante G. is the author of several books, including the best-selling *Mindfulness in Plain English,* which has been translated into a dozen languages. In 1996 he received the title of Chief Sangha Nayaka of North America, which means that he is this continent's highest-ranking monk of the Siyam Nikaya sect of Theravada Buddhism. He's also an avid health walker.

Andrew B. Howk will be attending Wabash College in Crawfordsville, Indiana. After he graduates he plans on attending law school but his specific career plans remain undecided. He continues to manage the Teen Buddhist Sangha which is now in its third year online with a growing and active membership. Andrew has been practicing Buddhism for four years but is not a member of any particular school of Buddhism. He enjoys learning about different cultures and religions through world travel, is a political/current event junky, reads religiously, and lives for just hanging out with his friends.

Myoju Meg Levie lives with her family at Green Gulch Farm Zen Center just north of San Francisco, California. In July 2003 she received ordination as a priest in the Soto Zen tradition from her teacher, Tenshin Reb Anderson Roshi.

Donna Lovong was born in Thailand near the border of Laos. She has a BA in sociology and is currently conducting public health research. She enjoys reading, traveling, and practicing eating meditation. She currently lives in Texas.

J. Marion is a student at the University of South Florida, majoring in religious studies. Some of her interests include dance and multi-cultural activities. Her Buddhist practice is in the Pure Land tradition.

Layla Mason is writing under a pseudonym.

Hilary Miller lives in California in a small town with many cows. She attends high school, which takes up much of her time, but manages to salvage some time in which to meditate, write, read, ride horseback, and sing in an all-girls choir. She is very grateful for the teachings of the Buddha, which have helped her to cope with depression, and firmly plans to continue practicing through high school and college and long after, until impermanence lays her in her coffin.

 **Kim Collins Moreno** grew up in Baltimore, Maryland. Childhood bouts with scarlet fever and pneumonia ensured that she would become bookish and unathletic. By fourth grade she had decided that she wanted to be a medieval studies scholar or an archaeologist when she grew up. She became an archivist and historian, which is pretty darn close and pays just as little. She works as an archivist for the State of Maryland and is pursuing her Master's degree in historical studies at University of Maryland. She lives in Baltimore with her husband. Kim has been practicing Zen for ten years.

 **Bhiksuni Thich Chan Chau Nghiem** (Kaira Lingo) is a nun in the Vietnamese Zen tradition of Thich Nhat Hanh. She ordained as a novice in 1999 and as a Bhiksuni in 2003. She has a BA and MA from Stanford University in anthropology. Sister Chau Nghiem lives in Plum Village, France. There she enjoys living deeply and mindfully with her many monastic sisters and brothers from all over the world. Together they practice arriving in the present moment with each breath and each step, as well as creating plays, composing songs and dances, canoeing, and joyfully engaging in a life of self-transformation and service.

Thich Nhat Hanh in his teens.

Zen master, poet, and peace and human rights activist **Thich Nhat Hanh** was born in central Vietnam in 1926 and joined the monkhood at the age of sixteen. He founded the School of Youth for Social Service, Van Hanh Buddhist University, and the Order of Interbeing. He has written over fifty books in English and was nominated by Dr. Martin Luther King Jr. for the Nobel Peace Prize in 1967. Thich Nhat Hanh lives in Plum Village, a meditation community he founded in France, where he teaches, writes, gardens, and leads retreats on the art of mindful living.

Kathleen Olesky at age 18.

Kathleen Millane Olesky has practiced Nichiren Buddhism for thirty-one years. Her husband and three children are all active practitioners and members of Soka Gakkai of America. She has been a regional leader for the New England organization for many years. Kathleen has a Master's in counseling psychology, an MFA in creative writing, and is certified as a writing workshop leader by the Amherst Writers and Artists. She lives in Newton, Massachusetts.

Maya Putra lives with her parents in Houston, Texas. She is involved in several social activities within her community such as the Tzu Chi Foundation (a non-profit organization dedicated to helping the needy), Student Environmental Art Council, film editor as well as camera operator at her local temple, and website manager for the Houston Indonesian Buddhist Association. Through her interest in film,

Maya hopes to make a difference in the world in a positive way. Maya is now a junior in high school for the Performing and Visual Arts, where she develops her creativity and art skills necessary in the field of filmmaking.

Anne Skuza, while born in New Jersey, spent the first five years of her life babbling incoherently in a strange combination of Polish and Ukrainian. At the age of eleven, Anne began studying Buddhism after a particularly fascinating assignment on world religions. Currently a sophomore at Mount Saint Mary Academy, Anne describes herself as "confused, but slowly progressing along the path to enlightenment." During her free time, Anne enjoys writing, playing Caesar III and The Sims on her laptop, and traveling the world.

Sumana Bhikkhu (Jake H. Davis) graduated from Marlboro College in 2003 with a degree in religion and applied linguistics. He continues to study and practice in the tradition of the Mahasi Sayadaw of Burma as well as interpreting for Burmese meditation masters in the U.S. and abroad. Jake's book *Strong Roots: Liberation Teachings of Mindfulness in North America* (Barre, Mass.: Dhamma Dana Publications, 2003) is freely available by post or for download from http://vijja.net/strongroots/. He was reordained as Sumanasiri on December 29, 2003, at 9:07 A.M. in Water Sima at the Panditarama Forest Center with Sayadaw U Pandita as his preceptor.

Lama Surya Das at age 25.

Lama Surya Das is a Western lama and Buddhist teacher, and founder of the Dzogchen Meditation Centers. He twice completed the traditional three-year, three-month Tibetan meditation retreat at his teacher's monastery cloister. Author of *Awakening the Buddha Within* and other best-selling books, Surya Das is a poet and translator, a regular columnist on Beliefnet.com, leads retreats around the world, and is active in interfaith dialogue. He lived in the Himalayas for fifteen years, and with the Dalai Lama founded the Western Buddhist Teachers Conferences. The Lama lives with his wife Kathy Peterson in Arlington, Massachusetts. His website is www.surya.org.

Tenzin Youdon Takshamtsang was born in Dharamsala, India, to a refugee Tibetan Buddhist family. She went to a strict boarding school in India where Buddhist teachings are followed daily. She came to the United States at the age of fifteen. Today, she is a junior at Lesley University in Cambridge, Massachusetts, majoring in business management. She is the founder and president of the Students for a Free Tibet chapter at Lesley, as well as a member of the board of the Lesley Buddhist Community. As part of the Tibetan dance troupe through the Boston Tibetan Association, she recently performed at Fleet Center in Boston in front of His Holiness the Dalai Lama. It was a great honor.

Alexis Trass was born and raised in Gary, Indiana. Formerly a junior high school teacher, she currently works as Associate Editor of *Living Buddhism* magazine, a monthly journal for the Soka Gakkai International-USA. She is a lifelong practitioner of Nichiren Buddhism and lives in Los Angeles.

Alan G. Wagner is a Ph.D. student at Harvard University, where he studies premodern Chinese Buddhism. He is interested in understanding Buddhist ethics in light of the claims of nonduality, with a particular focus on the Chan/Zen tradition. Alan lives with his wife, Helene, and their year-old son, Maxime; he enjoys screenwriting, jazz and world music, football, everything French, and travel to the far reaches of Asia.

Easton Waller is a Theravada Buddhist and a professor of comparative religion at Saint Leo University. He lives in Tampa, Florida, with his wife and three sons. Easton's works have been published in *Tricycle, Buddhadharma, Parabola,* and *New Thought,* as well as Wisdom Publication's *Nixon Under the Bodhi Tree and Other Works of Buddhist Fiction.*

Jeff Wilson is a member of the New York Buddhist Church. He currently resides in Chapel Hill, where he is pursuing a Ph.D. in religious studies at the University of North Carolina. He is also a contributing editor for *Tricycle: The Buddhist Review* and the website *Killing the Buddha*.

Venerable Yifa in college.

Venerable Yifa holds a Ph.D. in religious studies from Yale University (1996) and has been an ordained Buddhist nun since 1979. She studied law at National Taiwan University in Taipei. At the age of twenty, she received novice ordination at Fo Guang Shan at Kaohsiung, Taiwan. Fo Guang Shan sponsored her graduate studies, first at the University of Hawaii, where she received an MA in philosophy in 1990, and then at Yale. Within Fo Guang Shan, Yifa has served as an administrator of Buddhist universities and centers for the education of monastics, and as Provost of Hsi Lai University in Rosemead, California. She is the author of *Safeguarding the Heart: A Buddhist Response to Suffering and September 11* and *The Origins of Buddhist Monastic Codes in China*.

Jimmy Yu (Guogu) is a Ph.D. student in the Department of Religion at Princeton University, with a concentration in Chinese Buddhist history. He continues to study and practice in the tradition of Chan as taught by Master Sheng-yen. Among his many interests, Jimmy enjoys meditation and snowboarding.

About the Editor

 **Sumi Loundon,** 29, was born into and grew up for eight years in a Soto Zen community in rural New Hampshire. A fine arts major and religion minor at Williams College, she received a master's from Harvard University's Divinity School in 2001 with a focus in Buddhist Studies. Sumi is the editor of the anthology *Blue Jean Buddha: Voices of Young Buddhists* (Wisdom, 2001) and writes about young Buddhists in America and Asia for publications and conferences. For the last thirteen years, she has followed the Theravada vipassana lineage through the Insight Meditation Society in Barre, Massachusetts. Sumi is the Assistant Director at IMS' neighboring affiliate, the Barre Center for Buddhist Studies.

CONTACT INFORMATION

To contact any of the contributors or the editor, please send an email to bluejeanbuddha@hotmail.com or write to them, c/o Wisdom Publications, 199 Elm Street, Somerville, MA 02144 U.S.A. You may also visit the website www.bluejeanbuddha.org.

About Wisdom

Wisdom Publications publishes authentic Buddhist works for the benefit of all. Our titles include translations of the sutras and tantras, commentaries and teachings of past and contemporary Buddhist masters, and original works by the world's leading Buddhist scholars. Buddhism is a living philosophy and it is our commitment to preserve and transmit important works from all its major traditions.

To learn more about Wisdom, or to browse books online, visit www.wisdompubs.org.

If you'd like to receive our mail-order catalog, please write to this address:

Wisdom Publications
199 Elm Street
Somerville, Massachusetts 02144 USA
Telephone: (617) 776-7416 • Fax: (617) 776-7841
Email: info@wisdompubs.org • www.wisdompubs.org

The Wisdom Trust

As a nonprofit publisher, Wisdom Publications is dedicated to the publication of fine Dharma books for the benefit of all sentient beings and dependent upon the kindness and generosity of sponsors in order to do so. If you would like to make a donation to Wisdom, please do so through our Somerville office. If you would like to sponsor the publication of a book, please write or email us for more information.

Thank you.

Wisdom Publications is a nonprofit, charitable 501(c)(3) organization affiliated with the Foundation for the Preservation of the Mahayana Tradition (FPMT).